MW00768324

Diggin' For
TREASURE

jewels of hope when pressure & time collide

Feb 14, 2015

always look
in fire!

3Arleau Simm

GODZCHILD PUBLICATIONS

Copyright @ 2014 by Arlecia Simmons

Published by Godzchild Publications
a division of Godzchild, Inc.
22 Halleck St., Newark, NJ 07104
www.godzchildproductions.net

Printed in the United States of America 2014—First Edition
Cover Design by Ana Saunders of Es3lla ARTentional Designs

All rights reserved. Except as permitted under the U.S. Copyright Act
of 1976, this publication shall not be broadcast, rewritten, distributed,
or transmitted, electronically or copied, in any form, or stored in a
database or retrieval system, without prior written permission from
the author.

Library of Congress Cataloging-in-Publications Data
Diggin' For Treasure: Jewels of Hope When Pressure & Time
Collide/Arlecia Simmons

ISBN   978-0-9961043-8-8 (pbk.)

1. Simmons, Arlecia 2. Treasure 3. Hope 4. Faith 5. Jewel
6. Spirituality 7. Gullah 8. Charleston

Table of
CONTENTS

A Word from the Author

I n July 1998, I journeyed from Charleston, South Carolina, to Atlanta, Georgia, with a group of women to attend Bishop T.D. Jakes' Women Thou Art Loosed Conference. We did not make it out of the state before our bus broke down. We prayed and sang until the bus miraculously started back up and we continued on our way. We arrived late Friday night and found less than desirable hotel accommodations. Clean towels were in short supply and from the looks of the other guests, towels may have been unnecessary for their hourly stays. This trip is what we would simply call, "off the chain." I cannot say I recall Bishop Jakes' or Prophetess Juanita Bynum's sermons; however, I will never forget a moment that took place on our bus during a praise and worship/testimony period. It was in that moment that I spoke this book into existence. I spoke to the wind and shared with my sisters that I would write a book. Later in the day, a sister from my church, Francis, asked, "What's your book going to be about?" I could not answer that question at the time, as a subject or topic was yet to be determined.

I have been fixin' to write a book for years. I even wrote a short story later staged as a one-woman show, but the book spoken about in 1998 didn't come to fruition. Well, if I counted my master's thesis and dissertation, I could say I have authored two books, including several post-it notes multiplied and plastic bins overflowing with various ramblings and thoughts.

When we are given divine assignments, the enemy will make every effort to ensure that our mission is aborted and our dreams deferred. Even as faithful Christians, insecurity and procrastination will stop us in our tracks if we allow them to.

Years ago, I went into Barnes and Noble and began scanning the clearance table. Doubt and fear about my assignment triggered this thought: "What happens if my book ends up on the clearance table or in the dollar store?" That thought arose before I even prepared the manuscript. Prayer must counter these thoughts and faith must surface. It was faith that allowed me to walk into Waldenbooks, a major bookseller before online stores, locate the shelf where I envisioned my book, find the shelf with the S's, and place my hand where the "Si" selections were found. "My book will go here," I said as I ceremonially laid my hands on the section.

As I think back to that public confession made on a charter bus in 1998, I think of the impotent man whose story is recorded in John 5. The passage tells of a man who was sick for 38 years. There he lay, waiting for someone to place him in the pool where healing would annually occur after a "stirring" by the angel. Like that man, I, too, sat on the sidelines waiting for the opportune time to come. "Maybe a publisher will come by and put me in the publishing pool?" After a talk with Jesus, our Savior instructed the man to take up his mat and walk. Thankfully, it hasn't taken 38 years for me to receive my instructions to pick up my pen and write.

With a renewed mind, maturity, and wisdom, I dug for treasure and now share jewels found in the adventures of my 40 years of life!

"This is the LORD's doing; it is marvelous in our eyes"
Psalm 118:23

To my ancestors who prayed for me and my dreams

To my family and friends who have not extinguished my fire

INTRODUCTION

Walk into any jewelry store and you will find cases filled with fine jewels of varying clarity and weight. Amethysts, diamonds, emeralds and sapphires set in gold; silver and platinum await adoring children, eager fiancés, and remorseful spouses. An educated diamond buyer will not only consider the carat weight and clarity of a stone, but also the color and cut. Unlike the items available for purchase in a mall's food court, fine jewels were not prepared that morning or the night before. Rather, the "real" stones are the result of pressure and time. In most cases, miners risked their lives to unearth nature's gifts. Nowadays, companies are able to create synthetic gemstones. However, the stones with the most value are those that have endured the collision of pressure and time.

In our own lives, it is often after testing by the elements of illness, isolation, family drama, financial struggle, and rejection that we will experience the necessary pressure which aids in becoming the jewels God designed us to be. When we take some time to do some diggin', we unearth testimonies that amount to treasure. Or as my Gullah kin would say "tredjuh."

On the following pages, you will find what I call "jewels," which are devotional entries that will prayerfully encourage heavy hearts, challenge stagnant spirits, ignite laughter, and help you to begin the excavation process of discovering your own treasure.

I have dug through emails, journals, blog posts, and my memory to share with you 40 jewels for your journey. Enjoy and as always, look and live!

The Excavation Process:
How to Dig for Treasure as you Read

As the Holy Spirit has guided my re-encountering, reflecting, and writing, I pray you will receive a divine visitation as you read the following pages.

As you read, listen carefully. No, not to the rustling of the physical pages; rather, listen to how and where God is calling you into God's embrace, full disclosure, and healing.

Each jewel begins with a "Scriptural Meditation," which is a verse or passage that can be used during personal devotional time. The core of each jewel is the inspirational message, which prayerfully leads you into a moment of reflection. Each entry ends with three reflection questions for readers to explore individually or in community with other readers.

Write in the space provided or get a journal to chronicle your thoughts.

JEWEL 1

A Neighbor's Prayer
Scriptural Meditation: Philippians 2:4

Growing up in the Union Heights subdivision of North Charleston, South Carolina, our neighbors were like family members we spoke to throughout the day. For years, Charleston has been recognized as the Friendliest City by *Condé Nast Traveler*. "Wada people" like my Gullah kin rarely meet strangers. But through my travels over the years, I realize not everyone is familiar with our brand of Southern hospitality.

Most of my Iowa City neighbors may have likely never visited Charleston, so it wasn't long before I realized they didn't receive the memo that good neighbors say "Good Morning," "Hello," and smile or nod in passing. We were a global community, and daily I inhaled aromas of different lands and heard babies begin to speak in tongues needing translation.

The Bible has much to say about interactions between neighbors; however, rarely do some Christians remember Christ's Great Commandment in Matthew 22:39: "You shall love your neighbor as yourself."

How do people who believe they only share a geographic location love one another beyond a casual wave? How can I love someone who refuses to make eye contact with me and refuses to say "Hello"? How do I share the love of God with someone who doesn't embrace Jesus as Lord? We can spend our lives asking these questions, or we can spend our lives being the answer.

Interactions with some Iowa neighbors prompted me to ask the previous questions, then one night a neighbor became the answer. Prior to coming to the United States, she was a physician in Ghana and worked in ministry with her husband. I can't recall her name, but I can remember her sacrifice. The couple left their children with relatives in order for the husband to study public health with the hopes of returning to their own nation.

This woman worked for the university hospital, but could not practice medicine as she had once done in Ghana. She could no longer care for patients in the same way, but I found nothing prevented her from caring for souls.

We often exchanged greetings while walking or waiting on the campus bus, but one evening in the parking lot, our lives collided like never before. Darkness fell as we wrapped up what would be our final conversation as neighbors. "I'll be praying for you," she said. She then took my hands in hers and began to pray.

The power of God quickly fell as we stood in the Hawkeye Drive parking lot and she released words of assurance. She prayed for my feet, my hands, and for every assignment I would have in the future. In that moment, I knew something prophetic was taking place as she spoke as a Seer speaking on things I was petitioning God for and some events that would later occur. Tears fell as I could sense the washing of the Holy Spirit as her carefully paced words flowed.

Our neighbors may have been a little confused that night as we stood before God, but heaven was clear about our meeting. There was much anxiety in my body and mind as I considered the road ahead and prepared to move 1,200 miles to begin yet another faith walk. During my neighbor's prayer, I experienced peace and heard Jesus say "be still" to the winds and waves of my next move. Not only was I driving alone from Iowa to North Carolina to begin divinity school, but I was taking with me an unfinished dissertation and preparing to live in the basement of strangers.

On that August evening, the asphalt of the parking lot was holy ground, and a woman who likely felt the same anxiety when she moved thousands of miles away risked loving me, her neighbor.

REFLECTION QUESTIONS

1) How would you describe yourself as a neighbor? Would Jesus want to live next door to you?

2) How have you shared your faith with your neighbor(s)?

3) What are prayers you have offered on behalf of your neighbor(s)?

JEWEL 2

Reach Up!
Scriptural Meditation: Psalm 28: 1-2

Break your arm or cut your finger and you quickly realize the gift of your hands. Our hands swat flies and apply beauty supplies. With our hands, we express ourselves, give directives, and give God handclaps of praise. There is power in our hands. With raised hands, we can alert God about the trouble in our lives. Like an air traffic controller, we lift our hands directing God's attention to our problems.

In Psalm 28, the psalmist lifts his hands as an act of petition; summoning God to come and see about him. He reaches up to God in his distress. Yes, it's a place you've likely been in if you've lived in this world for more than a day.

"God, I have a problem, and if you don't attend to me, there's going to be a situation." I can hear David praying in Psalm 28. This ancient glimpse at life isn't as unique, as some of you know. At some point, you have found yourself feeling like you are going into a pit moment of disorientation. The pit is where you feel cut off from life, cut off from family, cut off from nourishment, and where you are left for dead. The pit can be a disorienting place.

Disorientation is that place some experienced when the federal government shut down in 2012. It's likely the place you were in when your best friend got killed in an accident. The place you found yourself in when you learned your child was on drugs, incarcerated, or would be born with a disability. This place where you likely could not say a word, but you had to wave your hands while praying. It is in a place of despair that the Psalmist realizes there is someone who can come to his rescue.

There are times in life when you will have to reach up. You might try to reach out for someone by phone, but they may not answer. You may use your hands to send a text message, or desire a communal response by updating your Facebook status or sending a Tweet. Depending on what else is trending, there may be no response. Crickets. Oh, but consider what would happen if you reached UP instead of OUT.

I once watched the cutest 15-month-old interacting with family and friends. There were words spoken with clarity and others not as coherent. She mumbled and wobbled as she tried to communicate her needs. She began to cry and whine, but when she saw her father enter the room she reached up. She was calmed after he reached down and picked her up.

When I saw the image, I was reminded how when I reach up, my Father who art in heaven will come through the door to see about me.

REFLECTION QUESTIONS

1) When trouble comes, to what/to whom do you reach out?

2) What stops you from reaching up to God in times of distress?

3) What disorienting things in your life currently need God's attention?

JEWEL 3

Holy Comedy
Scriptural Meditation: Genesis 21:1-7

Laughter is big business! Millionaires are made by the telling of a few good jokes. Their brands expand as they venture into books, television, and radio. With the various challenges of our families, communities and in this world, laughter serves as medicine. Like those before us, we find ourselves laughing to keep from crying.

In Genesis 17 there is a familiar story filled with a laughter that does not occur in a performing arts center. Rather, this holy comedy occurs in a tent by the oaks of Mamre.

No tickets were sold and the audience is small: Abraham, a 99-year-old fatherless man soon to be patriarch; his wife, Sarah, whose age similarly qualifies her to be Mother of the Church; and three divine visitors. A hospitable host, Abraham greets the visitors before the Holy Comedy show begins. Genesis 18:9-15 (NIV) reads:

9 "Where is your wife Sarah?" they asked him.
"There, in the tent," he said.
10 Then one of them said, "I will surely return to you about this time next year, and Sarah your wife will have a son." Now Sarah was listening at the entrance to the tent, which was behind him. 11 Abraham

and Sarah were already very old, and Sarah was past the age of child-bearing.12 So Sarah laughed to herself as she thought, "After I am worn out and my lord is old, will I now have this pleasure?"

13 Then the LORD said to Abraham, "Why did Sarah laugh and say, 'Will I really have a child, now that I am old?'14 Is anything too hard for the LORD? I will return to you at the appointed time next year, and Sarah will have a son."

15 Sarah was afraid, so she lied and said, "I did not laugh." But he said, "Yes, you did laugh."

Sarah had a tent, but maybe you are laughing from your bathroom. You have the promise of being a mother yet your last five pregnancies have ended in miscarriage.

Laughing because God said you were going to preach but you have never prayed in public.

Laughing because God said you were going to own a business, but your credit is so busted you can't afford to pay attention.

Laughing because God said you were fearfully and wonderfully made, but there's a man who beats you and tells you that you are ugly and not worth the dirt on his shoe.

You sit and you laugh because God must have jokes! The life you have isn't the life God promised you 5, 10, 15, 20, 25 years ago. You, the CREATED, laugh when you hear the plans of the Creator. The promise sounds so absurd you are bold enough to say: "God, you got jokes." But when God pulls the transcript to inquire about what you said, you answer: "No, God, I didn't say that; I didn't laugh."

Sarah is ready to use her AARP benefits and God is saying "Join Mocha Moms," a support group for stay-at-home mothers. She laughs.

Admit it, you have laughed. God asks you the question posed to her: "Is there anything too hard for God?"

Too much time has passed. Could the promise come to fruition? Laughing because you think you don't have what it takes to complete what God said in earlier chapters of your life.

Someone is laughing and saying: "God must have forgotten I am the wrong gender, height, color. God must have jokes and forgot I was born out of wedlock, and what he's asking me will require a two-parent household with 2.5 kids and a dog named Fluffy. We even join in the laughter of others as they doubt what God is doing in our lives.

In the end, Sarah's doubt is turned into sweet laughter as she embraces the child called Isaac. Beloved, God's name isn't on the marquee of the Comedy House and God's promises are not jokes written to open a concert. God is able to do the miraculous in your life, your ministry, and your home.

REFLECTION QUESTIONS

1) What has caused you to doubt the promises of God?

2) How do you respond when you hear others talk about accomplishing what sounds like impossible goals?

3) Recall a time when God has made you laugh by fulfilling a promise you earlier doubted.

JEWEL 4

Expectant Celebrations
Scriptural Meditation: Psalm 37:4

I am forever grateful for an imagination. During childhood, our imaginations transported us to faraway places. Or sometimes they resulted in bruises when the superhero powers in our minds did not activate before encountering the edge of a bed. As children, many believed they could fly like Superman or soar above the heavens. Sadly, we are told to "grow up" and exchange our imagined powers for rules and established programs.

For some of us, our vivid imaginations were not left behind or suppressed. One day while cooking and listening to music on Pandora, I began to envision how I would dance to a Michael Jackson tune in my wedding dress. "Note to self: A detachable train is a must. Scratch that, your equilibrium is off and you'll need another reception dress," I told myself.

I sashayed, swayed, wobbled, and dropped it like it was warm envisioning the party at my wedding reception. It was a glorious time. Another day, I heard Sam Cooke's "Darling, You Send Me." Oh, yeah, that one is going on the playlist, too, I said audibly as I shopped.

At the time of this writing, I had not dated in 10 months. So what's all of this talk about adding tracks to a wedding playlist and a synchronized dance with my father? Well, in the words of faith given by the Apostle Paul in Romans 4:17, "I speak those things that have yet to exist as if they are alive or in existence." I haven't seen the husband, but I can see the DJ in the corner taking over the music when the band takes a break. I know this kind of imagination can be dangerous because it can force you to take risks that take you away from the known. This type of visioning silences fear, statistics, naysayers, and anything counter to what you have heard in your own spirit.

It is easy to discard your dreams and visions because the last time you held one, you did not see it come to fruition. You believed God gave you this vision and placed a desire in your heart, yet there was no manifestation.

Yes, I have been there. However, I have also been on the receiving end of exceeding and abundant blessings. Some days after what was once a goal comes to fruition, I find myself asking, "Did I really do that? Did I really apply and get into Duke? Did I really move to Iowa? Did I really…? And then when all of the questions are asked, I am reminded, "Yes, you did it all with the help of the Lord. " Oprah Winfrey has said, "God can dream a bigger dream for you than you could ever dream for yourself."

It's a dream where Cupid's shuffle gathers wedding guests on the dance floor after they have feasted on shrimp and grits and other Lowcountry fare.

REFLECTION QUESTIONS

1) What's the biggest dream you have ever dreamed?

2) How has fear killed your dreams?

3) Has God shown you any new dreams about the future? If so, what are they?

JEWEL 5

Puppies and Shortcuts
Scriptural Meditation: Jeremiah 33:3

You get what you pay for! We may learn this the hard way when we focus on bargains or cut corners. I am a sucker for a good deal, but I have learned some deals are too good to be true.

Because "kitchen beauticians" are common in my community, having my hair done at someone's home instead of in a beauty salon is not an uncommon endeavor. Many braiders or stylists who work from their homes have formal training while some are self-trained. Their prices are usually more affordable, but it's likely the encounter will provide some form of free excitement.

I should have discerned a new encounter would be an adventure since my referral was a guy who tried to pick me up in a Chinese restaurant. Instead of getting my number, I got the number for the woman who had recently retwisted his locs.

When I first called the woman, I heard puppies in the background. "They'll be out of the way," she responded when I inquired about their location. Cost and time were set, but I couldn't stop thinking about the dogs I had heard. The appointment was set for my hair to be done the day before my departure to Northern Uganda.

As I entered the duplex apartment, the lingering odor from a recent party filled my nostrils. No judgments or worries. Well, I couldn't keep that vow for too long. "Arff, arfff, arff." Puppies.

Yes, puppies caged in a bedroom with the hair dryer. Oh, but they were not alone. A woman holding a 2-month-old baby sat under the dryer as the 5 or 6 pit bulls barked nonstop "Oh, my gawd; I have to get out of here," I thought as I considered how I could escape without just telling the woman "this is some foolishness up in here." As I waited for her to finish up with a woman holding a baby in the room with the puppies, I tried to figure out how to leave. I left for Uganda the next day, so I was in a fix. Saving money, huh?

I texted a friend: "Call me ASAP and tell me to come and pick u up." Lord, I lied, but I needed to escape this situation before she started on my hair. "I am ready for you," she said, summoning me into the room with the dogs. Not only were my nerves not feeling the non-stop barking, but my asthma and allergies were not interested.

"Could you do it in here?" I asked while standing in the living room area. Hey, we were not working with too many rules here. Why not? Meanwhile, I was still waiting for Kendra to call for my escape. Still no reply text or call. She looked at the hair products I brought, and then went to answer a knock at the door.

"Can you pay me now? My stepdad has to pay a bill," she says. I quickly took the money out of the purse clutched tightly on my lap and handed her the money. The extra $5 for styling was out of the question, it was my service charge for this distress. Meanwhile, my hair was still undone and Kendra could not be found.

"When is Kendra going to call?" I thought, holding the phone and waiting for an incoming call or text message.

As she began to separate my locs – something told me to wash my hair before arriving – Kendra finally called. "Heyyyyyyy, sooooooooo, yeah-hhhhhh," Kendra says trying to detect whether I was safe. "Hi, oh, you need me to pick you up? Ohhhhhh, my, she just started on my hair," I responded trying not to laugh at myself.

To avoid going back into the room with the dogs, I told her I would just let the sun dry my hair. While I saved about $35 that day, I paid the difference with my emotions. I couldn't even be all spiritual and ask why God had allowed me to end up in such a situation when I willingly entered into this in-house kennel-turned-beauty shop.

I tell this story as a reminder of how we can get into "question-able" or unhealthy situations when we decide to take shortcuts. While I couldn't afford to get my hair done before and after visiting Uganda, I took a shortcut which could have proven more dangerous than I origi-nally thought. As the saying goes, "God takes care of babies and fools." On that day in the home beauty shop/kennel, I truly felt like the latter.

REFLECTION QUESTIONS

1) What shortcuts have you taken that were costly?

2) How have you "paid" in the end for things that appeared less expensive in the beginning?

3) What did you learn the last time you tried to save money or time, but found you spent more of each?

JEWEL 6

I Know I've Been Changed
Scriptural Meditation: Acts 22:6-11

As a cub newspaper reporter in Eden, North Carolina, I ventured daily to the Eden Police Department to retrieve reports of incidents that occurred overnight. After determining which reports were newsworthy and not simple violations, the clerk took a black marker and blotted out information about victims, suspects, or investigations. Louise, who was always friendly and welcoming, would redact information the police department or the law deemed inappropriate for public knowledge. Thus, I could not report information that interfered with an investigation or revealed information about a victim. With a black marker, those details were instantly removed. If only our past worked that way.

Although God may redact our past indiscretions, others may keep a roster of what some call "B.C." or "Before Christ" days when Jesus was not the one for whom you lived, breathed and had your being. No matter how much God may be working in your life now, others may have hard drives with stored memories of your past indiscretions.

"Your nuggets of inspiration are both inspiring and entertaining, even if they come from a mind and lips that were not always so kind," read the e-mail I received from a friend responding to one of my weekly "Doses of Inspiration." Before establishing a blog, I distributed weekly inspirations via email.

I was always excited to read the responses to my inspirations, but this message ignited a number of different emotions. I will have to admit that I immediately felt a sense of defeat and shame. I began to question myself and this new writing ministry.

"Can the once quintessential mean girl now spew words of encouragement?" I asked myself.

I was frustrated for a matter of minutes before God sent me a spiritual e-mail: I can make all things new! Receiving that nice-nasty email about my past indiscretions and existing transformation alerted me that a true shift was taking place in my life and ministry. I later realized God was preparing me to enter a space where tough skin and courage were needed. I was being challenged to go forward even if my past wanted to hold me hostage.

Are you refusing to go forward because the adversary keeps reminding you of your past? Have you stopped moving forward because of what "they" might say?

Instead of acknowledging what you have overcome and thanking God for your deliverance, have you chosen to go into the C.P.P., the Christian Protection Program? The C.P.P. doesn't require a physical relocation, but you choose to bind and store up your gifts because you are afraid someone might find out about your past. You deem yourself unqualified to serve your church, community, or even the PTA because of what someone might say if they knew about your past.

Growing up, the senior choir at the New Hope Missionary Baptist Church sang a song titled "Jesus Dropped the Charges" by the O'Neal Twins. The selection would make people shout. As a child, I didn't understand why the song made the older people "catch the Holy Ghost." I now realize the song's power rested on its proclamation of God's grace. "Case dismissed, case dismissed; saved by grace."

Because of Christ's shed blood on a cross at Calvary, my file has been redacted; allowing a once mean girl to encourage others to look and live!

REFLECTION QUESTIONS

1) How have you judged others based on their past?

2) How does God use you in spite of you?

3) What is God calling you to do, but your past keeps getting in the way?

JEWEL 7

The Legacy of Faith
Scriptural Meditation: Hebrews 11:1-2

Black History Month celebrations at the New Hope Missionary Baptist Church were epic! They were always executed with a cultural awareness of both local and global histories. My deceased friend, Minister Kelvin Grant, was often the visionary behind our dramatic presentations. We re-enacted historical moments or the narratives of living and departed heroes and heroines of the race before jubilantly singing "Lift Every Voice and Sing."

The faith of our ancestors is one of the most important gifts to have and hold dear, yet it is often overlooked. Many of the names of those who prayed for a better life and world are not in history books, yet their prayers were recorded in heaven. As slaves and free persons, they prayed their children and children's children would experience the sweetness of liberty and justice. Even with scarred bodies and souls, they dreamt and hoped for brighter futures for future generations.

During the early 20th Century, my relatives worked as domestics and oyster shuckers on St. Helena Island, South Carolina. These Gullah people who trace their roots back to the Tom Fripp Plantation, spent days opening oyster shells and transferring the mollusks into buckets. My sanctified imagination leads me to believe other actions took place during that messy and cumbersome task. Without written evidence or an oral account, I believe someone prayed for me. With aching hands and soiled clothes, they whispered supplications to God on behalf of their "chillun." I envision they called on the "Lawd" for this "lil gal" here.

"I am the hope and the dream of the slave," Mother Maya Angelou wrote in her poem "Still I Rise." Yes, she was one of those personalities we talked about at New Hope. On May 28, 2014, Mother Angelou transitioned from labor to reward and joined the ancestors who gave us a firm foundation. They have written visions that we can now run with into the future.

I have revised their scripts while honoring the original narrative. Even with letters before and after my name, "I be who I be" because somebody prayed for me. I am the testimony and good report of oyster shuckers who "rabbled dey mout" and prayed.

REFLECTION QUESTIONS

1) How has your family's faith influenced you?

2) How do you honor your ancestors?

3) What are the blessings in your life connected to those who came before you?

JEWEL 8

Why Go It Alone?

Scriptural Meditation: Psalm 55:22 and I Peter 5:7

Once while exiting an airplane, I noticed a woman behind me struggling with her bags and an agitated baby. Her accent and dress suggested she was from a distant land, but her problems were not foreign to me. Often, I find myself physically overloaded and carrying more items than I can bear. Sometimes, even emotionally, I carry burdens I don't have enough money to fix or knowledge to think through.

This fellow passenger attempted to carry her baby, their belongings, and retrieve something from the overhead bin. The baby was hanging on for dear life. Even his small, chubby face indicated that something wasn't quite right. As expected, passengers behind her were irritated. Some had connections to make while others were simply ready to deplane.

I turned back and extended my hands. Without exchanging a word, she released the child into my arms. He willingly reached for me and held on to my shirt as we exited the cabin. It only took the mother a few minutes to pull herself together and retrieve the little fella. This mother simply needed a little help.

Like that woman, some of us are carrying heavy loads. We often try to go it alone when help is available. That mother recognized she needed help, so she accepted it when offered. Like her, I was a sojourner who could offer assistance on her journey. I didn't need to know her life's story, I just needed to be available to offer the necessary aid needed in that moment.

Society tells us we must be strong and show no signs of weakness. Think back to the time you struggled in school when tutors were available to help, or the time you moved and packed up an entire home by yourself because you believed no one would lend a helping hand. You struggled with childcare while not accepting the help of the grandmother at church. And even when physical help was extended, we struggled to cast our cares on God who offers to help carry our loads. Like the fellow passenger on the airplane, no questions are asked, but hands are extended.

Can you recall the lyrics to the old hymn "What a Friend We Have in Jesus"? Verse two reminds us: "Oh what peace we often forfeit, O what needless pain we bear, all because we do not carry everything to God in prayer." God hears our humble cries and answers them in ways we least expect. Through prayer we release our heavy loads into the arms of the one who is the sustainer of our lives.

Other travelers may have expected the flight attendant to offer assistance, but God sent another traveler on the journey. No matter the load, help is available and is on the way.

REFLECTION QUESTIONS

1) What loads are you carrying alone?

2) Why have you decided to carry the load alone?

3) How can you assist others carrying loads of weight and responsibility?

JEWEL 9

A Pepperoni Testimony
Scriptural Meditation: Joshua 4:1-24

Walking through the freezer section of any grocery store gives me flashbacks involving frozen pizza, a portable oven, and a trip to the doctor. One summer while in college, I was contracted to serve frozen pizza and distribute coupons in the freezer section of a grocery store. I burnt myself on the portable oven, and became ill after two days of standing in the refrigerated area. I may have made about $100 for the two-day stint that ended with a doctor's visit and a bout of congestion. These days, I can't even walk past the frozen food section without wanting to cough.

We often forget about those experiences in our lives that definitely made us stronger, even if they almost killed us. We murmur and complain daily about our finances, jobs, and personal lives without taking a step back to remember how far God has brought us.

In Joshua 4, it is recorded that, after the Israelites had crossed over the Jordan River, Joshua commanded a representative from each of the twelve tribes of Israel to retrieve a stone from the riverbed. These stones of remembrance would remind their children how God dried up the Jordan for their ancestors.

For me, the memory of a grocer's freezer section is a reminder of how God has not allowed my hustles to take me out. For so many in the United States, hazardous jobs are the norm and we forget the danger that workers subject themselves to in order to care for their families. Just consider the food we waste, and the farmers, growers, harvesters who must wake up early, go to bed late, and use dangerous equipment to ensure fresh food arrives on our tables.

We are so quick to develop amnesia in an attempt to forget about all of the experiences that were not comfortable or glamorous. Yet, those experiences can help us appreciate not only the sacrifices made by others, but also remind us of the experiences that have built character in us.

While being a temporary food merchandiser wasn't all it was cracked up to be, my "Pepperoni Testimony" is a stone of remembrance I now carry with me on the journey.

REFLECTION QUESTIONS

1) What artifacts or memories serve as "stones" of remembrance for you?

2) What lessons are attached to your stones?

3) What stones should be discarded because they reflect memories of pain instead of hope?

JEWEL 10

Bent but Not Broken
Scriptural Meditation: 2 Corinthians 4:8-10

The people who handle us day-to-day rarely know our stories. They know our names and what we share on social media, but they rarely know who "our people be." They may know you are strong, yet they don't realize how your strength was developed. They may see your sun-kissed skin, yet not realize that slavery was not the start or ending to your story. Thankfully, some people have more knowledge of our complete stories.

"You are the descendent of the ones who chose to live," said my clergy sister Kesha during one of our Iowa conversations where I was ready to kiss the Hawkeye state goodbye. This woman of God, who was a native of South Carolina and attended college in Chicago, understood the various challenges I faced. When we talked, she reminded me that not only was I a woman of faith, but I was a woman with the blood of Gullah men and women flowing through my body. Men and women who survived the Middle Passage; lived through violence on the plantations; witnessed lynchings; worked in fields and factories; and still managed to lead abundant lives in unsuitable living environments.

Kesha reminded me I was the descendant of people who were from the loins of those who decided not to jump during their journeys from the coasts of West Africa and the West Indies. People who chose to survive the work of the Tom Fripp plantation. People who chose not to take the knives they used to shuck oysters to kill themselves, but decided to run on to see what the end would be. Somewhere down in their sanctified souls, they realized trouble would not last always. They kept the faith and endured.

When I get frustrated about life and what it is or is not at the time, I close my eyes and think back to those who fought and were left with visible wounds. Because of their endurance and God's grace, I have to keep moving. For those who could not attend school or attended segregated ones when allowed, I must continue to fight through the process of academic hoops.

Even with isms, glass ceilings, and workplace discrimination in varying forms, we must continue to stay the course, keep the faith, and envision a time when those behind us will not experience the same struggles.

Prayerfully, those behind us will call us faithful.

REFLECTION QUESTIONS

1) How and where did you grow up? Were you ever ashamed of your background? If so, why?

2) Why were you afraid of "who you be" or "who your people be"?

3) How do you work to better appreciate your background and events which helped to shape you?

JEWEL 11

What's in Your Arsenal?
Scriptural Meditation: Deuteronomy 8:18

It is amazing how during every season of our lives, God allows us to obtain skills we can make use of later. We walk around complaining about things we don't have when what we need is actually at arm's length, if we only take inventory of our arsenals.

As a toddler, while most children were watching *Sesame Street*, I was getting dressed for work. That's right. I escorted my maternal grandmother in her Nova as we rode around selling Stanley Home Products.

I guess I was able to develop some analytical skills early, as I was responsible for assisting with inventory and packaging. "Lecia, remind me to take Ms. Johnson a Degreaser on the first of the month." I would nod as we drove to the next home or business, listening to her talk about people, products, or what we would later have for dinner. In the car or on someone's porch she would write out receipts, often calculating the tax in her head.

During her 28-year sales career as a Stanley Home Products rep, she also dabbled in Tupperware, Avon, ceramics, and chocolate candy. I was always amazed by how she could sell people things they did not realize they needed or wanted. "Emma, this product here will get that stain out of that couch over there. Get me a wet rag so I can show you." She would go to scrubbing and Ms. Emma would proceed to get her change purse to pay. Even to this day, I think she could sell the sun a light bulb.

Like many young black children growing up in the South during the 1930s and 40s, my grandmother did not finish high school. However, Louise didn't let that stop her from achieving success. She used her smile, the gift of gab, and the persuasive spirit God placed in her arsenal. Instead of lamenting about opportunities, she found a way to use those skills and talents to impact her church, community, and home.

I will admit I've found myself giving a laundry list of requests to God about what I need to be successful. "And if you can connect me to this person, then they can do this…" In some instances, those prayers would be answered with specific needs; other times, I heard "You already have what you need."

REFLECTION QUESTIONS

1) What skills or talents have you allowed to go untapped?

2) Are there things in your arsenal you should spend more time developing?

3) What experience from your past, once considered negative, is now working together for your good?

JEWEL 12

I Hope You Dance
Scriptural Meditation: Psalm 150:4

D r. Dorothy Perry Thompson was one of the few African-American professors at my undergraduate alma mater, Winthrop University. The English professor and poet was a "power to the people" kind of sister. I never considered pursuing an academic career prior to meeting her, but seeing her at graduations sparked my interest in the academy. Dr. Thompson displayed her African pride on campus and during formal ceremonies. It was not hard to pick Dr. Thompson out of the crowd at a commencement service, as she adorned her black doctoral gown with kente cloth and an African kufe hat replaced her mortar board. I recall saying to myself, "If I ever become a professor, I am going to be like Dr. Thompson."

That same uniqueness was expressed during Dr. Thompson's funeral in January 2002. Dr. Thompson's physical body succumbed to cancer at the age of 57, but her spirit lives on. In the process of mourning her death, I was reminded how to live. During the eulogy, the pastor recited passages from Isaiah, Hebrews, and I Corinthians while weaving in Maya Angelou's "Phenomenal Woman." He also used one of the plants near the pulpit to pour a libation. Attendees laughed through tears as a friend described Dr. Thompson's various exploits and her love of dance.

That day, no one talked about how many books or poems she had published or how many degrees she had earned; the focus was on celebrating the life that was exuberantly lived. Dr. Thompson returned to the earth dressed as a regal African queen.

As I walked out of the Walls A.M.E. Zion Church and greeted my former classmates and professors, I realized that I needed to "turn up the volume of my life." I realized I needed to dance more, to live more, and to love more. So many people have forgotten how to dance. For some, the music stopped abruptly or a once broken toe took longer to heal and never returned to the dance floor.

Dr. Thompson's home going service reminded me I wanted to dance and dance and dance, so when it was time for me to return to the Lord, my family and friends would laugh through the tears as they recalled a phenomenal life lived!

(REFLECTION QUESTIONS)

1) Describe an event that could cause you to stop dancing?

2) What has interrupted your dance?

3) What do you pray will happen so you can begin to dance again?

JEWEL 13

Budget Reform
Scriptural Meditation: Genesis 41:25-27

My mother and her siblings often laugh at how their mother managed to feed the family of seven with one box of chicken from the Dee Dex Snack Bar, a black owned business that provided fast food to African-Americans before they could eat at other restaurants in Charleston. When recounting that childhood memory, it often sounded as if they could still taste the crispiness of the chicken as they talked about my grandmother's mastery of distribution. "We all ate and were satisfied, but we still don't know how there was enough meat to go around!"

Workers in my generation make more money in three months than some of our elders made annually. They fed and clothed children, bought land, and supported their entire household on incomes we couldn't fathom. Although the cost of living has changed, hearing their testimonies is often convicting if you consider how they were able to do so much with so little.

Whether distributing money or food, the steward of each must strategically allocate to ensure that needs are met. The verb "allocate" means to "give" or "earmark something." The divine instruction baffled me until I read Genesis 41. In that passage, you find Joseph interpreting Pharaoh's dreams, which foretold of seasons of abundance and famine. But Joseph doesn't stop there. He instructs Pharaoh on how to allocate and store resources during the season of abundance in an effort to prepare the nation for an approaching crisis.

So often, we fail to realize the value of our money and time until we are out of both. Have you ever withdrawn money from the bank and within a matter of hours or days you cannot even account for your spending? You are guessing you enjoyed whatever you purchased, but could now use a tank of gas.

A woman preparing to retire before age 60 gave me one of the best pieces of advice I have ever received. For a number of years, her annual salary was $60,000, but each year, she resolved to live off of half of what she earned. At an early age, she learned how to strategically allocate resources in preparation for a future season.

In addition to your financial resources, consider how you are spending your life's resources. Are you spending too much time consumed with other people's problems? Do you spend more time on the phone gossiping than you do cleaning your physical and/or emotional home? Is your checkbook balanced? Have you exercised at least once this week? Have you planned for the lean days that might be ahead?

Lord, help me to allocate appropriately so that I am prepared when the season changes!

REFLECTION QUESTIONS

1) What areas of your life are in need of reallocation?

2) What area of your life is experiencing a deficit? Why?

3) What is the first step you can take to begin to balance things out (personally, professionally, and spiritually)?

JEWEL 14

When Women Serve
Scriptural Meditation: Joel 2:28-29

Before accepting my call to ministry, I immersed myself in reading about women in the Bible and in contemporary ministry. My dissertation research, which I usually bore people to death talking about, is a study of the life and work of an Iowa woman who was ordained in 1930 in Missouri. Although she was active within a local Western Iowa church, she "pastored" via radio for more than 50 years. While there is an ongoing debate about the role of women in ministry, God has always used his daughters to spread the Gospel and assist with the maintenance of the Church.

In my childhood church, there were two female ministers whose life impacted me more than I realized. In the fall of 2007, I was saddened to learn that Rev. Mary Broomfield and Evangelist Mable Maxwell, had gone home to be with the Lord. About two months before Evangelist Maxwell's transition, I called the 91-year-old to check-in. Her mind was strong, as she provided updates on her grandchildren, the great-grands and other relatives I could not recall. As our conversation ended, she thanked me for calling and said, "You stay on the King's highway." That was a Word!

As a child, I suffered from an extreme case of eczema that caused me to miss months of school. Because Mary Ford Elementary had limited air conditioning, I did not spend many spring days in the classroom. Teachers visited my home to drop off assignments and go over new material. That is, when I was not hospitalized for weeks. While most children would remember missing recess, I recall Rev. Broomfield and Mrs. Mary Lee Fields, the pastor's wife, coming over to pray and rub me down with oils and other concoctions they learned about from friends or the health food store. My grandmother, Louise, would be right there with the tag team as they prayed, sang, and greased me down. You name products used for cooking, disinfecting, and skin lubrication, and it's likely they used them. Rev. Broomfield always arrived like she was ready to do battle. If my illness was attached to some kind of demon, she was prepared to take that demon out and let God arise.

When the three women prayed, the whatnots in the living room rattled as they prayed and believed God for my healing. I am grateful these women were not just Sunday saints, but they were true disciples of Christ who did good works like Mother Dorcas in Acts 9.

Although Mothers Broomfield and Fields have gone to be with the Lord, I can still sense their praying hands on me. I can still see Maxwell sitting in her living room praying over a bottle of olive oil I used to anoint my home. Whether she was alone or gathered with one or two, she faithfully guided the church's prayer meeting until physically unable to do so.

As I continue to stumble along the King's Highway, I keep walking, praying, and being about the Father's business because I know that Rev. Broomfield, Evangelist Maxwell, and Mrs. Mary Lee are in that great cloud of witnesses cheering me on and encouraging me along the way.

REFLECTION QUESTIONS

1) What words of encouragement have you received from praying women?

2) How has a church or community elder helped fortify your faith?

3) Speak and list the names of the spiritual mothers and fathers on your journey. How can you pay their efforts forward?

JEWEL 15

Are You Not Much Better?
Scriptural Meditation: Matthew 6:25-26

One Iowa winter morning, I looked out of my living room window and as far as my natural eye could see, ice and snow blanketed the earth. It was February. It had snowed every week since Thanksgiving. As I stood there thinking about my upcoming schedule, the possibility of having to cancel an engagement due to the weather, the five extra pounds lingering since the holidays, and the uncertain status of some relationships, I noticed a bird flying near the bush outside my neighbors' window. Not all birds migrate, as these resident black birds made daily visits to this bird feeder under my window.

While drivers and walkers were slipping and sliding, the birds kept singing as they navigated through the winds, rain, and snow.

As I gazed out the window, I considered a few verses from Matthew 6:26-27 (NIV): " Look at the birds of the air; they do not sow or reap or store away in barns, and yet your heavenly Father feeds them. Are you not much more valuable than they? Can any one of you by worrying add a single hour to your life?" Sometimes we have to ask ourselves, "Am I not much better than the birds?"

No thought?

Does that mean you must ignore the thread of bill payment reminders in your email? Does that mean you can stop ignoring the phone calls from your student loan collection service? Well, you must decide how to responsibly respond to the personal debt incurred; however you can do so with a clearer understanding of your true source: God.

God is your source.

If you can, go outside and look up. Can you spot a bird? Both of you were created by God. If God provided in seasons past, then fly high and watch God do it again.

REFLECTION QUESTIONS

1) In recent weeks, what physical need has consumed you?

2) Why is it so difficult to trust God like the fowl of the air?

3) How has God spoken to you about being a conduit of provision?

JEWEL 16

Barefoot Bullies

Scriptural Meditation: Matthew 6:14

"Ee gon dye wit ee shoe on."

The saying is one I hear Gullah people use when pronouncing judgment on someone who has committed crimes or acts thought unforgiveable. It's always been a perplexing adage because good, well-meaning people die with their shoes on. But what I've taken this to mean is because of the wrong done, the one who has wronged will possibly die tragically without the peace of transitioning in a comfortable state. Death will come so quickly, there will be no time to be undressed or call in family and friends to supply comfort in the final minutes of transition.

I wondered if the boy at the bus stop lived, or had he died with his shoes on. He should be a 40-something year-old man now, but back then he was a middle school boy. To this day, I'm not sure what I said to him, or if I looked at him the wrong way. I just recall the blow that made my nose bleed at the bus stop in the apartment complex where I lived with my mother after we left the nest of my grandparents' home.

While others bullied me with their words, he used his fist. I'm not sure if this was before or after my grandfather drove across the bridge daily to monitor the bullies. For some reason, I'm not sure if I even told my mother about the incident. She likely would have visited his mother to discuss the matter. I wiped the blood from my nose and went to school as planned.

But did he die with his shoes on? Did he even finish high school? Did he grow into a man who now abuses his wife? Is he a better man than the boy I knew on that day?

Can I honestly say I have forgiven that sucker who took his fist and used it on my face?

I wondered what I would do if I ever saw him again. Likely, he would say "Hey, girl, I haven't seen you since middle school." And I would act like I'm completely delivered and ask how he was doing and if he had children. Yes, the Reverend Doctor would be civil and nice, but could I offer forgiveness? Although I lived to tell the story about this incident, the pain and embarrassment of that day remains.

For those who have ever been bullied at school, work, or even home, the wounds of your bullies' acts are deep even after scabs form; even after your bully relocates, graduates, or signs the divorce papers.

Do you forgive or do you continue to wonder whether they died with their shoes on?

Extending forgiveness is one of those areas on a Christian's journey where the proverbial rubber must meet the road. We are challenged to love those we feel don't deserve our love. Then we read the words of Jesus found in John 13:34 (NIV): "Love one another. As I have loved you, so you must love one another."

For Christians, the command is to love those who don't deserve our forgiveness for the pushing, teasing, and violence inflicted. Truth be told, we don't deserve God's love after we have pushed, teased, lied, stolen, and transgressed in various ways. Yet, God loved us enough to send his only begotten son while we were bullying others.

If I did not know how Jesus dealt with his bullies, I would spend my life looking for the boy from the bus stop. Because I am short, I could run, jump, thump him in the throat, and then run away. However, I'm clear paying him back is not what Jesus would have me do. No, that would not bring God glory.

When you think of your bullies, consider what took place on Golgotha. When Jesus Christ hung on the cross between two thieves, he could have summoned warring angels to take all of his executioners out. Instead Luke 23:34 reports Jesus saying, "Father, forgive them, for they do not know what they are doing."

REFLECTION QUESTIONS

1) How has someone extended forgiveness to you?

2) Why is it hard for you to forgive the bullies in your life?

3) What could be your first step toward forgiving someone who wronged you?

JEWEL 17

I thank you, Lord!
Scriptural Meditation: 1 Thessalonians 5:18

Good old fashioned testimony services are now rare in the opening liturgies of many church services. Saints auditioning for *Sunday Best*, time limits due to multiple services, and a generation desiring microwave services have influenced the removal of testimony periods. However, all of that is dismissed at least one time a year when congregations gather for Watch Night. The service which normally takes place in African-American churches of various traditions commemorates how enslaved blacks worshipped the night before the Emancipation Proclamation went into effect. The descendants of those freed continue to gather on the evening of December 31 to sing and testify about how they made it over.

Oh, I've given a testimony a time or two. One year, my testimony may have sounded like an audition tape for Iyanla Vanzant's *Fix My Life* show. During that season, my "daddy issues" got the best of me, and the saints were asked to "pray my strength in the Lord." Now, I just shake my head thinking back to that night and the genuine pain felt.

Even in the midst of the laments and complaints that inch their way into testimonies, the highlight of most narratives is a pronouncement of gratitude.

"If I had 10,000 tongues I couldn't thank Him enough," a mother or father of the church would say after "First giving honor to God who is the head of my life." I never quite understood that phrase when the seasoned saints would declare those words; that is, until I received abundant blessings that I, too, could not ask, think, or imagine.

Frustration and pain desire to mute our voices of praise, but we have to declare the rocks will not cry out for us. The rocks cannot communicate the joy I get thinking about everything God has done for me. I am thankful for every valley, as they have taught me to appreciate the mountains.

I am thankful for the summer floods, as they taught me to appreciate God's earth.

I am thankful for every relationship that dissolved, as they taught me to value the unions that remain.

I am thankful for every ache and pain, as they taught me to appreciate health and insurance.

I am thankful for every prayer, as I know angels are dispatched on my behalf.

I am thankful for those who love me, as they teach me how to love.

I say "thank you" when I walk into worship because I am glad to be in the number just one more time. Somewhere in the world there is a Christian praying and worshiping God in secret. While we are clapping, singing, and running up and down the aisles, believers in distant lands pray huddled in darkness.

.   "You have missed your shout," if you are waiting for Watch Night service to thank God for what God has done for you, just today. Not yesterday or last week, just today! New mercies!

I know it seems hard to be thankful when there is trouble on every side, but if you can feel the press of the trouble, you're still in the number.

REFLECTION QUESTIONS

1) You have been given two minutes to testify. Tell it! What is your testimony?

2) Have you ever felt as if you could not share your testimony with others because of fear of jealousy or judgment? If so, why?

3) Beyond verbally sharing your testimony with others, how can you express your gratitude for the blessings you have received?

JEWEL 18

Jesus Take the Wheel
Scriptural Meditation: Psalm 55:22

The morning of the driving test was filled with anxiety. The new employees gathered for our drivers' training and were then broken up into groups. Our instructor, who looked like she was barely old enough for a learner's permit, gave us a few instructions before my group departed for its road test. I was the third driver up.

"Good," she said as I merged onto Interstate 80. Within a matter of seconds, I saw two eighteen wheelers in the mirror. As the third driver up that morning, I asked Jesus to take the wheel. Oh, the petition may have even been audible when a doe wondered near the exit as I approached the Interstate. Deer in Iowa frolicked both day and night. The wind blew and I prayed. I kept my foot on the gas and continued praying before seeing two big trucks coming down the interstate.

"The blood of Jesus," is what I repeated while watching the trucks ignore the strong winds. The other staffers were casually chatting while riding as if all was well. Maybe it was in their world, but driving this mammoth white van was creating stress for me. Driving anything larger than a compact car was not the norm, but my summer job as an instructor required certification to drive a state van. By God's grace and protection, I received my motor pool clearance. The only field trips my class took were walking ones.

In life, there are people driving or navigating through situations that are too big to handle. Your wind may be a disobedient child, or money that is always funny. Maybe it is a dysfunctional relationship. But, the more you try to work it out or drive, the more you swerve. And just when you think you've found your exit, your passengers distract you. You have missed your exit, you end up delayed, and you feel like you may never reach your destination. Have you considered asking Jesus to take the wheel? I have come to realize that there are some circumstances in my life that I cannot navigate in the natural. If I am going to live to tell about it, then I will have to fast and pray.

What is it today that would compare with eighteen wheelers that could run you off the road? An ill loved one? A broken relationship? A season of depression? Sickness in your body? A stalled career? Or, could it be financial woes of any kind? Some may find more money more problems.

Ask God to take control over every situation that is too big for you to handle alone. That day in the van, God was in control of the situation, but I still had to keep my hands on the steering wheel and my foot on the gas.

1) If you compared your problem to a vehicle you had trouble driving, what does the 18-wheeler riding alongside you represent? What are the challenges to your challenges?

2) What does surrendering control of a situation look like for you?

3) Why is it that we call on others before we call on God?

JEWEL 19

Celebrate the Season You Are In

Scriptural Meditation: Ecclesiastes 3:1-18

I once had lunch with an expectant mother whose baby was due within a few weeks. "I hope she comes early," she said, explaining a premature delivery would accommodate the beginning of the academic schedule. You can rub your belly, walk the mall 20 times, and say "come out, little person" and babies past their expected arrival may remain in the comforts of the womb until medical intervention takes place. With natural births, babies arrive when, and only when, it is the divinely appointed time.

I believe it is the same process for the seasons of our lives.

If we had our druthers, we would fast-forward some of the scenes in our lives, including (but not limited to) the difficult seasons of marriage, illness, or work-related issues. Long suffering is one of the fruit of the spirit we could truly live without. Yet, televangelists and even our local pastors and spiritual advisors are constantly reminding us that it is our season. We hear: "It's your season for overflow." "Walk into your season!" "It's a new season."

As I look back over my life, I consider how all of the seasons I have transitioned through prepared me for today. We often desire to rush through seasons not realizing that those are our times of reconstruction and transformation. In high school, many couldn't wait to graduate and begin college. After entering college, we couldn't wait to step into the "real world." Then, we found ourselves savoring the memories of what some told us would be the "best days of our lives." Next came the countdowns to our 25th, 30th, 40th, and 50th birthdays; only to one day tell people we are one age and holding!

There are some seasons we prefer over others. You hope some seasons will never shift; yet there are others you could live without. The one you are in now may be uncomfortable, unproductive, or even not understandable, but it's the season you have been assigned. Remember, seasons change.

Even if you are experiencing a season of lack, all things will work together for your good (Romans 8:28). Think back to the times where you felt alone, hopeless, or discouraged. What did those seasons teach you? Did your faith increase? Can you see how Go was executing a master plan?

Global warming may attempt to confuse us about the weather in the earth realm, but know that God is in control of the seasons of our lives.

1) Do you recall a season in your life when you were anxious about next steps?

2) Did you rest in that season or spend more time hoping for its expiration?

3) What actions have you taken during past seasons of waiting?

JEWEL 20

Blessed to be a Blessing

Scriptural Meditation: Genesis 12: 2-3

Appeals during church offerings can be rather interesting as ministers and church leaders remind congregants of the stewardship God expects. "Give until it hurts," admonished one church leader as ushers came forth with offering plates. Giving when it is inconvenient or uncomfortable could be what he was suggesting, but what about giving until even you are confused? You know, that time you offered to pay a bill for someone when your own light bill was on a payment plan. What about the day you bought someone's lunch when your own children needed dinner? Yes, that kind of sacrificial giving that makes no sense and is not witnessed before a congregation.

How would it feel if you were in a position to be the provider of a blessing instead of the recipient? We have all heard of the philanthropy of Oprah, Bill Cosby, Bill Gates, and others. Have you ever considered that you could also be blessed to be a blessing?

Years ago, an Iowa couple donated $2 million to provide housing for families whose loved ones were in the local hospital. Then there is the woman from Indiana, who after receiving a legal settlement, gave her favorite waitress $10,000 to assist with college expenses. The woman whose daughter and husband had died said, "I saw a need and I knew I could fill it."

For someone, a need might be a bag of groceries while someone else just needs a tank of gas until payday. One day I heard God say give someone $25. "Okay, God, if you say so." While I am sure I could have used the money to pay on one of my many bills, I did as instructed. I wrote a check and gave the female minister a $25 check. Later she told me that she debated coming to church that morning because the gas it took to get to church was the gas she needed to go to work the next day. She decided to come to church and trust God who then used me to meet her need.

Are there needs you can meet? Can God trust you to meet a need? You may not be able to write a check for thousands or hundreds of dollars, but consider how your gift of time and talent could bless today. You do not have to have millions or thousands of dollars to be a blessing; God will honor our small gifts when they are released with a cheerful heart. As a college student, I'll forever be grateful for those $3 handshakes from the mothers in the church. Back then, $3 could get you a half tank of gas. Many had never stepped foot on a college campus, but they could sow into my dreams.

Some of the seasoned saints blessed others without needing credit for their gifts. Their fists and handshakes were tight as they encouraged you to "do good," "take care of yourself," and "be safe on that road." They didn't need everyone in their business; they just wanted God to be pleased.

According to 2 Corinthians 9:10, God gives seed to the sower! Do you have seed in the ground, or have you only been on the receiving end of all benevolence?

REFLECTION QUESTIONS

1) What does your current level of giving to your church, nonprofits, or others say about you as a giver?

2) Why does it sometimes feel difficult to give?

3) In what ways could you bless others this week?

JEWEL 21

No Delays or Cancelled Itineraries

Scriptural Meditation: Psalm 119:60

Harlem Renaissance writer Langston Hughes posed the question: "What happens to dreams deferred?" Hughes was not the first person to ponder the human will as Solomon advises in Proverbs 13:12: "Hope deferred maketh the heart sick; but when the desire cometh it is a tree of life."

Often I hear people talk about what they are "fixin" or "fitna" to do with a plan whose implementation is years out. "I'll do it when… I retire, send the kids to college, graduate from college, go back to school, find a husband or wife, buy a house, and get my money right," blah, blah, blah..."

"Long life ain't promised," I've heard my elders say. A quick look at any newspaper's obituary page will reaffirm this. On any given day, you can find a notice for an infant or toddler who has succumbed to illness; a teenager killed in an accident; a baby boomer whose life was snatched by cancer; or a great-grandparent whose eyes simply went dim. While the page is often filled with narratives of people who have lived long and somewhat fruitful lives, there are also those who never quite got to their to-do lists.

On each obituary page, there is a death announcement for someone who spent their entire life saying: "One of these days!" The baker who could have taken out any challenger on *Cupcake Wars* will never be known for his could-be-world's-famous recipe because of fear. After learning how to bake while spending summers with his grandmother, he spent most of his life hiding his love of the kitchen because of perceived gender roles. Yes, on special occasions he baked a cake, but to become a cupcake artist would be considered asinine. Instead of stirring batter and piping out designs received in his dreams, he used his hands in the manufacturing industry. To make the time go by, he mentally combined ingredients and created new cake flavors. Oh, but those mouthwatering flavors would never meet the palates of brides on their wedding days or children at birthday parties. Sadly, the recipes he never attempted died with him.

What is it that you've been putting off because of fear or until life becomes less complicated? What has deferred this dream?

With or without a cheerleader, know God has assigned us tasks that we must attempt to accomplish before leaving this earth. Sometimes you will have to be like David of the Bible and encourage yourself. Reading God's word in Scripture will provide you with the reinforcement you will need for the journey. Embrace passages like Philippians 4:13 "I can do all things through him who gives me strength."

Will you wait another month, year, or decade to accomplish what your hands have been assigned to do? Continue to walk in your blessings, and pray that God will give you whatever resources are needed to stir up the gifts placed within you!

REFLECTION QUESTIONS

1) What is one step you can take today to bring a dream to fruition?

2) What has deferred your dreams or goals?

3) What is one thing you believe you must accomplish before leaving this earth?

JEWEL 22

Great is Thy Faithfulness
Scriptural Meditation: Lamentations 3:22-23

One of my favorite hymns is "Great is Thy Faithfulness." Sometimes all I need is one verse to stir my soul. Sometimes, one verse might be all I can recall without a hymnal. I can encourage myself by simply humming: "Morning by morning new mercies I see…"

These new mercies aren't seen with physical eyes, but are experienced in a myriad of ways. I receive new mercies when I leave home for the day, only to realize the front door of my house was not only unlocked but open all night. New mercies when you realize a burner on your gas stove was left on all night, but you woke up to turn it off.

Whether we wake up each day and acknowledge God's new mercies or we find ourselves disappointed, once again, with the actions of others, God has a way of whispering to us, "I am faithful." Oh, yes God is. I am grateful that God is not as shady as I am some days.

Sadly, our experiences with family and friends factor into a relationship with a God we believe but cannot see. Maybe it is the significant other who says one thing and does another. It could be the child who promises to behave in school, but then comes home with a note from the teacher. It could be the friend who says, "Girl, I'm going to call you right back." That call may never come, or it may appear when a favor or a monetary loan is needed. Oftentimes, we expect very little from others. Yet we would like to assume people will honor their commitments or vows.

I am grateful "God is not a man that He should lie" (Numbers 23:19). And while God's promises may not come to fruition right away, everything willed for our lives will come to pass. "The haters can't cancel your dreams," I told a congregation while preaching on the life of Joseph. God is faithful even when others are not.

If we are to walk in integrity, we must consider that people will not always remember what we say, but they will remember what we do. God's faithfulness should challenge us to consider our integrity and the mercy we extend to others.

REFLECTION QUESTIONS

1) How has God been faithful to you?

2) What are areas in your life requiring more faithfulness on your part?

3) What are some characteristics in people whom you identify as faithful?

JEWEL 23

Gabriel Has Not Retired
Scriptural Meditation: Luke 1:26-28

On Oct. 9, 2007, I went to my Iowa City, Iowa, mailbox and found the strangest thing. The carrier was still there as I retrieved my mail. "I'm not sure what happened with that," he said as I looked at an envelope mailed from Charleston, South Carolina, on Dec. 20, 2006. It was properly addressed and contained a Christmas photo card from a college friend. Someone had placed a slash mark across my address and wrote "moved." Not only had I not moved, but I had lived at the same residence for two years. The postal workers had become accustomed to my name and knew I was a South Carolinian, yet that envelope had circulated for nearly 10 months.

The envelope was properly addressed with correct postage and was anticipated, yet it arrived in a season beyond the one intended. Because we had exchanged Christmas cards for the past 11 years, I began to wonder if something had happened with our relationship. We often played the game "Who will send out their cards first?" But that year, no card was received. It was mailed, but not received as scheduled. Friends often laugh that they record my address in pencil because of my many moves, but everyone knew there was only one Iowa address. Still, no card. In life, we may have a tendency to think God has forgotten about us when the messages we seek are delayed. We wait and wait, and may begin to think "Did God forget about me?" "Is something wrong with our relationship?" "Did God forget exactly where I am?"

Even when the U.S. Postal Service or UPS cannot locate you, God knows where you are.

The all-knowing God has not forgotten where you live, and can still send a word to change your life. That is what happened to Mary, the mother of Jesus who unexpectedly received the very first Christmas greeting: "Do not be afraid, Mary; you have found favor with God. You will conceive and give birth to a son, and you are to call him Jesus. He will be great and will be called the Son of the Most High. The Lord God will give him the throne of his father David, and he will reign over Jacob's descendants forever; his kingdom will never end." (Luke 1: 30-33)

After 400 years of silence, God spoke through Gabriel with a message for both Mary and Israel. God knew exactly where to dispatch Gabriel to give Mary her divine assignment. Neither an address change nor weather conditions could delay God's word from reaching the virgin who was only preparing to say yes to the dress.

During the 10 months while my Christmas card circulated, I kept going back to my mailbox. Just because one piece of mail didn't arrive did not mean the postal worker stopped delivering. Daily I returned to see what else had been sent, whether gift or bill.

Like Mary, there are messages you don't even know are coming your way. On the way are prophetic words that will confirm life-changing events. The Holy Spirit will come upon you, so wait and know that Gabriel has not retired.

REFLECTION QUESTIONS

1) What word are you waiting for God to send your way?

2) How do you open yourself up to receive God's word for your life?

3) When do you most question if God has forgotten your address?

JEWEL 24

Spared to Serve
Scriptural Meditation: John 15:16

Y ou are on this earth for a reason! Yes, you! There is a reason you are alive, breathing, clothed, and in your right mind. Some days, the rightness of our minds is negotiable, but we work with what we have. But seriously, think back to the times when God blocked your premature departure from this life.

When I am in Charleston, driving down Ashley River Road at the corner of Carriage Lane, I think about the time in high school when I almost rolled out of a moving car to avoid being raped. Thankfully, when I opened the door and said I was about to jump, the young man realized I was serious and shouted "I'm taking you home." Even when some of our bad decisions could have led to destruction, because of God's grace, we were not consumed.

Each time my car rolls across a railroad track, I think about the night my life could have ended some 20 or so years ago. During my senior year of high school, I befriended a number of other students during our participation in a cotillion. As friendships developed beyond the event, we stayed in contact after graduation and during the early years of college.

One night during a holiday break, we loaded up a car to find a party about 30 miles away from home. After driving to the location where no party was found, we decided to return home. During the drive we debated and laughed before realizing we had crossed a set of railroad tracks with no warning signal. As we rolled across the tracks, we all looked to the right only to see, but not hear, a train approaching. There was no whistle or alert, and if we had tarried on the tracks seconds longer, there could have been a collision.

While I focus on looking and living, I often think back to that night and all of the potential in the car. Others have had similar experiences, but didn't live to tell about the time their car almost collided with a train. Others threatened to jump out of moving cars, and likely jumped or were subsequently raped. On both occasions, God's mercy overrode the enemy's plans.

I am not sure if anyone else ever told their parents about that night--I know I didn't. What I know for sure is somebody was praying. I later realized why parents are so strict when it comes to their children venturing out. Whether spiritual or non-spiritual, parents desire to protect them from hurt, harm, or danger. While parents don't often articulate it, they are also attempting to protect their children's futures.

Those incidents in my teens reminded me that there was a reason I was spared from death and destruction. I had more work to do. There is a reason you are still here! You have more work to do. No, not the jobs or careers attached to our direct deposits and medical benefits, but those assignments uniquely designed for us even before our parents found our names in magazines and in song lyrics.

Finding your assignment in the earth may be a tedious process. Some people realize what they were called to do in childhood, and they may become nurses, teachers, or other professionals they dreamed about for years. For others, there is experimentation, waiting, and frustration. But even when your call is not that obvious, look in the mirror and say "I have work to do." Ask God to direct you to the work you have been assigned.

That night as we rolled across the railroad tracks, beside me sat a friend who is now an Obstetrician and Gynecologist. I am not aware of what she says as she delivers babies into the world, but if ever she finds herself short on words, she can tell them, "You have work to do."

REFLECTION QUESTIONS

1) Has there been an incident you believe you were spared from because of a greater purpose?

2) If you could be completely transparent, what would you say is the reason you are here on earth?

3) What has God shown you about your future that scares you?

JEWEL 25

Faith on Fumes
On a Rainy Day

Scriptural Meditation: Deuteronomy 31:8

After a few miles on a mini road trip, I realized that I hadn't checked the weather report. A dark cloud in the sky reminded me that I'd forgotten to consult with weather.com. I kept driving and clearly heard the Holy Spirit: "There are times I won't allow you to check weather conditions because what you find may convince you to never leave for your journey." I realized this talk wasn't just about the summer rain or approaching storm.

When you are fixated on the "weather conditions" more than on the journey, you become distracted by the clouds, storms, and winds. You become discouraged if there is not 100 percent sunshine in the forecast. I have learned that weather conditions aren't always the best. But if you want to make it to your destination, you have to keep accelerating. A rain cloud may hover over a few miles of the journey, but keep driving. I have pulled off at an exit or rest stop while Mother Nature had her way, but I kept moving. That's what happened in the car, but on an academic journey, I pulled off by taking fewer hours one semester until a storm subsided. When the rains were too powerful, I eased up on the gas. Oh, I have had experiences where the rain never stopped. But I had to keep going if I wanted to make it to my destination.

In addition to not checking the weather, I also didn't assess my financial resources. I had ¼ a tank of gas for my 44 mile journey. Make that 88 miles roundtrip. I opened my wallet and discovered five one dollar bills. Well, with gas at $3.10 per gallon, $5 was more like a snack for my thirsty gas tank.

"God, I will have to trust you to get there and back."

If push came all the way to shove, I had an active AAA premium account. My deceased maternal grandfather, who often fussed about less than half a tank of gas in my car, would not be pleased.

Driving away from the gas station and considering the limits of my fuel, I realized this wasn't the first journey I had started with limited resources.

In 1999, before resigning from my job to attend graduate school, I sat at my desk asking God how I could make the next move with limited resources. "God, I have $7 in my savings account. How in the world am I going to quit my job, move away, and go to school full time?"

How could I leave the known for the unknown?

With my 25-year-old faith, I realized this is what they called a "faith walk."

I took the GRE and in secrecy applied to the graduate program. After waiting on a response, I was accepted into the program. I moved 110 miles away, worked odd jobs, took out loans, graduated, and returned months later to accept a Best Thesis Award.

While the road wasn't easy, God remained faithful when I didn't allow the limits of my resources to stop me from taking the journey. Before the second week of school, I was awarded a graduate assistantship which came with a stipend and covered a portion of tuition. If I didn't make the first step by applying and pursuing the degree, then God couldn't work all the things together for my good.

God already knew my limitations!

Trust me, when it's a God idea, God will take the two fish and five loaves in your life and pay tuition, open the business, complete the cross country move, and perform miracles beyond what you could ever imagine when you proceed with more faith and less fear.

(REFLECTION QUESTIONS)

1) When have life's storms convinced you to delay a journey you needed to take?

2) When have you trusted God's strength would be made perfect in your weakness?

3) How do you know when something is a good idea or a God idea?

JEWEL 26

Sitting at our Mothers' Feet

Scriptural Meditation: Proverbs 31:26

As a child, I was blessed to spend time with sassy, seasoned, and settled female members of my village. I never saw the inside of a daycare, so I spent my early days with my maternal grandmother and aunts. When I was old enough to leave the house alone, I spent time down the street at Ms. Vick's house. While she had grandchildren who visited, some days I would sit with Ms. Vick on her porch. She didn't talk much, but she was there to listen to my nonstop dialogue. "Yep, they are letting me go to a special program this summer." She'd just nod, fan, and keep listening.

When I really wanted to talk, I ventured across the yard to Mrs. Daisy's house. I don't really know how old she was, but we were girls. I will admit I had an ulterior motive when I visited Mrs. Daisy: lemon frosted cookies. I was always offered a lemon cookie and something to drink as we sat at her kitchen table and chatted. I could only imagine what I was talking about at 5 and 6 years old. The first time I experienced the grief associated with death was when Mrs. Daisy died. She was my friend who listened to my stories and had scrumptious cookies.

When I wasn't making solo visits, I was with my grandmother visiting the homes of other women as she sold Stanley Home Products. We visited women in their homes, workplaces, and sat on many porches. I would sit and listen as my grandmother tried to sell furniture polish while also discussing life and advising the women on their problems. And when we weren't on someone else's porch, someone like Ms. Cordray was sitting on ours. She traveled with a towel and continuously wiped her sweat as she and my grandmother talked.

Before it had a name, I was learning about the Prison Industrial Complex and its impact on families in my community.

Just thinking about the many summer days I spent in the presence of women making ways out of no way, reminded me how significant those times were. I was learning the art of listening, support, and friendship.

In the second chapter of Titus, Paul instructs Titus to teach the older women so they can teach the younger women among them. For some feminists or womanists, there may be some tension with this text. However, no matter how you exegete the verses, Titus 2:3-5 shouldn't be completely dismissed.

These days, some church women believe teaching must come from their current experiences, or what I consider the sanitized versions of their lives. However, daughters may benefit from hearing the story before you were saved, sanctified, and filled with the Holy Ghost. You know, when you were out in them streets. The single mother who comes to church with three children and no man in sight may not connect with the women behind the white suit. She may not feel so uncomfortable if she knew the white suit covered a woman who was once a single mother with four children who had three fathers. But what if the seasoned woman shared words of encouragement with that young mother who feels like she is alone?

Oh, I know some will say that they have a new identity in Christ and old things are passed away. But just imagine how the redacted files of your life can help those behind you.

Recently, I had an interesting discussion that reminded me why talks like the ones I am suggesting are needed in our churches and families. "She needs to stop having all of them chern (children)," said the grandmother about a granddaughter. "We'll, why don't you talk with her?" I asked the woman who had parented many children alone. She shook her head. "She won't listen to me."

I left that conversation saddened, believing the cycle of single parenting in some families could be prevented if generations interacted more. Of course, this woman's story was on display as children never knew fathers and grandchildren never knew grandfathers. How could sharing her story of love and loss help her grandchildren?

What would happen if instead of being reactive, we were proactive by sharing our journeys with the young women and men in our lives?

Instead of sitting in the corner of the barber shop waiting for your turn, how could you encourage your brother when he's talking about his anxieties?

Some have asked: Who will help us? Who will save us? Maybe the answers and balm needed within our churches, communities, and families already exists in the mouths and stories of others.

1) Where do you gather your wisdom?

2) What is one piece of advice from a seasoned member of your community that you are known to repeat?

3) Which lesson(s), learned from elders, do you still embrace?

JEWEL 27

Who Are You Representin'?
Scriptural Meditation: 2 Corinthians 3:2-3

People are often amazed to learn that I am a member of a sorority. "You never wear t-shirts or anything," they say. Someone once picked up my car keys and commented: "You don't even have a keychain." I believe exhibiting my sorority affiliation is a little like displaying one's faith. Televangelist Joyce Meyer has one of the most comical illustrations on this matter when she ministers about people with their Jesus bumper stickers and pins. You do not have to advertise when you "live it." I am an educated woman who is service minded and doing work to protect the welfare of others, so I represent my sorority without the shirts, jackets, and other paraphernalia.

I now own a "Jesus is my BFF" shirt, but it's likely I may wear it one day when others may question our relationship. At times, we miss the mark and others may question our witness. One day, I had to repent after "cutting a fool" with a lab tech who was attempting to "handle me" after a four-hour doctor's visit that included x-rays and lab work. Low blood sugar and hunger may not be acceptable excuses for that mean eye I gave that day. One of the lab workers grabbed me a cup of juice, as she realized that drawing blood was not going to help the situation. I was one grumpy little woman, and I was not a very good epistle to read in that moment. Later that evening, I realized that my actions did not reflect who I was representing. I was not acting like Jesus' BFF. Rather, I had tainted my witness by allowing my natural state to override my spiritual state.

People will judge us by what we say and do whether we wear crosses around our necks; "What Would Jesus Do?" bracelets on our wrists; or choose to only wear skirts to indicate our sanctification. They will listen more carefully to our words, watch our facial expressions, and monitor our actions to determine our legitimacy.

There have been times in secular settings when strangers have said to me: "There's something different about you." It is my prayer that the difference they noticed is the light of Christ. May that difference point people to the one who came to change our identities and make all things new.

REFLECTION QUESTIONS

1) What kind of text do people translate when they see your life? Are you translated as a novel, a tabloid, or a devotional?

2) How have your interactions with someone factored into how you viewed their Christian witness?

3) What will you hope people will say after an encounter with you?

JEWEL 28

Wing Lifters
Scriptural Meditation: Exodus 17:11-13

A clergy sister calls two friends from seminary her "Aaron" and "Hur." The reference to their relationship is based on the Exodus account where the two men were instrumental in aiding in the Israelites' battle against the Amalekites. "As long as Moses held up the staff in his hand, the Israelites had the advantage. But whenever he dropped his hand, the Amalekites gained the advantage," reads Exodus 17: 11.

When Moses' arms became tired and he could no longer hold them up, Aaron and Hur came to the rescue, located a stone to support his body, and stood by to support his arms. They held him up. They fortified Moses's situation. They didn't just conspire to see who could take his place, but they supported him until victory was won.

In a contemporary culture where we can quickly unfriend, unfollow, and block callers, having emotional, spiritual, and physical support are all blessing we often take for granted.

While some people are very comfortable with friends who know how to have a good time and offer little criticism, some of us need Aaronesha to challenge or question us about recent decisions. We need Hurmeana to "push back" on what we have determined is "truth." We need people we can trust to offer both affirmation as well as critique. This process is not all warm and fuzzy. Rather, it may come with some undesired feedback as well as accountability.

You know, real accountability requires you to mean what you say and say what you mean! You need people who even hold our words accountable, expecting us to speak well of ourselves and God when our lips desire to speak defeat and lament.

After a time of table fellowship with two of my sisters, we began a time of "iron sharpening." We challenged one another about current realities and offered possibilities never envisioned. After discussing everything from theology to hair care all while watching a streaming church service, I pulled out my laptop and summoned them to listen.
"I want to share a few pages from my book; tell me what you think."

But first, they wanted to know how the book was setup, and how I had come up with the concept. They wanted to know more about my targeted audience. They wanted to know what any reader of an unknown author might want to know.

I read the passages in my "good NPR voice" as one friend noted. "Read that again," said one as I finished with the reflection questions of each section. "Ummm, read that last question again?" Silence.
"That last one doesn't go with what you just read us. You went from one concept to another."

I read the question over and over again. Delete. What do you suggest?

"Why not ask ... ?"

Awwww, I like!

I continued to read as they listened attentively. There were head nods, smiles, and "What you talking about, Willis?" looks offered. I was blessed with a safe space to be artistically naked and unashamed. Before readers look at the page with confusion, I was able to share the words I have spent many years pondering in my heart. I was even challenged to consider the possibility of communal reading and how I could help facilitate the process.

While I often write in isolation, I was grateful for having my literary arms lifted by my Aaronesha and Hurmeana. I left that night and could say "I got this!"

REFLECTION QUESTIONS

1) What are the best attributes of your support team?

2) What kinds of support do you offer others?

3) What are areas of your life where supporters are needed?

JEWEL 29

I Trust God with Me
Scriptural Meditation: Psalm 71

As a little girl, I remember my grandmother religiously watching the *PTL Club* on television. I did not attend daycare, so Jim and Tammy Faye Bakker had more credibility with me than Bert and Ernie.

In July 2007, I was saddened to learn Tammy Faye passed away after a long battle with cancer. While most people will attach her legacy to the PTL scandal of the late 1980s, I will forever remember a statement she made while appearing on the *Larry King Show* a few days before her death. Based on her physical appearance that evening, the Gullah people would say that she had already started "traveling." In essence, she was making her transition to be with the Lord. However, when King questioned her about her faith in God, she boldly said: "I trust God with me."

"Wow!" I said to myself. The death angel was sitting at the foot of her bed and here she is proclaiming God is still faithful.

It is easy for us to put our trust in so many things in this world, but we often lack the faith to trust the one who said, "Let there be..." Those three words orchestrated the creation of heaven, earth, sky, land, and all of the things we have come to know. In the creation account found in Genesis 1, God entrusted humans with creation.

Even from the beginning, people have trusted other things and people more than they trusted God.

We go to the doctor's office and trust physicians will administer the proper care and prescribe the proper medication. We trust others to adhere to handwashing practices while caring for us, yet we hear of increased infections transmitted from provider to patient. We eat at restaurants where we trust employees have adhered to posted signs reminding them to wash their hands. You might trust they have complied, but I am going to say grace over my food and all of the utensils somebody accidentally dropped on the floor! (I was a burger girl long before I was a writer!)

Some of us will rely on a complete stranger to tell us how to invest our life savings, yet some will not trust their local church with their tithes and offerings.

Is it fair to say you trust others more than you trust God? The old saints would say, "Sometimes you have to trust God when you can't trace him." Even when I can't sense God's presence or touch, I choose to trust God with me!

(REFLECTION QUESTIONS)

1) What areas of your life do you find it difficult to release to God?

2) Why is it so hard to trust God?

3) When have you found yourself trusting in people more than you did in God?

JEWEL 30

Nile River Miracles
Scriptural Meditation: Psalm 27:5

In July 2011, I journeyed through Northern Uganda on the Pilgrimage of Paine and Hope with a group of seven Americans, a group of young Ugandans, and a couple living in Tanzania. We finally made it to Kampala after flying from Raleigh, N.C. to New York, then to Brussels, and then a quick stop in Rwanda.

It didn't take long before the adventures started! "Oh, Lord! I just gave the man my bag!"

"Who? Who? Which, man? Where did he go?"

After a few minutes of confusion upon our arrival, all bodies and luggage were quickly accounted for as the four African-American seminarians and four Caucasian Christians met our fellow pilgrims.

As our bus rolled away from the airport, it was dark. But if I had trusted God to board an airplane and journey across oceans, I had to trust God in the midst of this darkness. While I thought I would be afraid to sleep in my new environment, I slept in the twin bed like I was back at granny's house on Union Heights.

"This is Holy Ground," said Father Emmanuel Katongole, Ph.D., as we stood in the backyard of a convent in Kampala. I removed my sandals. After Father Emmanuel had offered his opening remarks, I began to sing as previously requested. "We are standing on Holy Ground and I know that there are angels all around…" After a few seconds, the others joined in. "Thank the Lord, everyone knows this one," I thought in that moment.

As we sojourned along the Nile River on our 10-day excursion, our bus approached a slippery slope after an afternoon rain. One wheel was wedged on a cliff. Some men nearby and some pilgrims got off the bus in an effort to push the bus back on the road. But not everyone could exit the bus; some of us needed to stay to maintain the weight of the vehicle.

I stayed with the two young Ugandan women and a senior male pilgrim. The two women were calm and began to sing as I prayed "Jesus, Jesus, Jesus, the blood of Jesus, Jesus, Jesus." Tears streamed down my face as I considered the bus could possibly slide off the cliff. While I was terrified, I considered my death would be in the Nile River. Not just any place, but in the Nile where Moses was placed as a baby.

The two women began to sing: "May the Spirit of the Lord, come down, Amen; may the Spirit of the Lord come down, may now power of the Lord from heaven come down, may the power of the Lord come down; May the protection of the Lord come down, Amen." I finally joined in, realizing it was time for my faith to activate.

With rain slapping their faces and mud covering their bodies, those outside finally rocked the bus back on the road. The power of the Lord had come down. The God who hovered over me on the backroads of South Carolina when I traveled as an evangelist was the same God overlooking the bus on the Nile River.

Later that day during our time of reflection, I realized the two women were able to remain calm because these kinds of mudslides were normal in Uganda. In addition to driving conditions, there were areas of their lives that remained on the edge.

"Oh, Arlecia don't cry," they said during those minutes of terror. For them, too many tears had likely already been shed. May God forever help us remember those whose lives include proverbial mudslides daily. May the protection of the Lord come down, Amen.

REFLECTION QUESTIONS

1) What were the slippery slopes of your life where you realized God intervened?

2) What are the songs of comfort and invocation that help you overcome your fears?

3) Who are the people who can encourage you in the midst of trouble?

JEWEL 31

Don't Change Your Name, Change Your Perspective
Scriptural Meditation: Ruth 1:19-20

Mother Naomi. Her story in the book of Ruth is a narrative that I've wrestled with for many years. "My man and my chern gone," my Gullah imagination could hear her say as she urged Ruth to go about her business as she returned to Bethlehem.

It is a passage often preached on Women's Days, and one used to inspire single women to hang on for their divine placement in "the field." "I'm waiting on my Boaz," the saved, single women proclaim. Oh, we shout, as Ruth finds favor with Boaz and secures a marriage proposal. This praise break of Ruth's successful gleaning endeavor often masks the pain captured in Ruth 1 where we find an aging Naomi possessing little hope. She is bitter!

This bitterness is not foreign to many of you. We are people living in a fallen world where circumstances and situations ignite bitterness within us. If you listed the reasons for your bitterness, the following areas may be identified:

- Abandonment by a friend, parent, partner, spouse
- Infertility; the loss of a child
- Death of parents and loved ones
- Involuntary singleness
- Health challenges; disease
- The loss of a job; loss of possessions
- Abuse and physical threats

The list could go on and on and on and on, and like Naomi, we may consider "the hand of the Lord is gone against [us]" (Ruth 1:13). Even as I confront my own singleness, an item on the above list, I pray: "Lord, I don't want to be bitter."

You have seen living, breathing bitterness with your own eyes. Remember Sue, Jimmy's ex-wife? He left her for another woman in 1981, and Sue continues to make society pay for Jimmy's sins. She is cantankerous and everyone experiences her wrath. Sue has worked three jobs to raise her two children. Both of the kids have completed college, yet Sue is still bitter about what Jimmy did in 1981. For some of you, she sits one cubicle away. For others, she is the church sister who attempts to micromanage God, the pastor and all parties in between. Is there a small part of Sue in you? Are you Sue?

While deliverance is available to Sue and Jimmy, who left Sue, but has been bitter for 20 years about paying child support and alimony, they may never receive the gift of healing that is available.

If we keep reading beyond Ruth 1, we realize that instead of remaining bitter, Naomi mentors Ruth who secures a more prosperous future for both of them. Because of her mentoring, they were able to stay alive. God wants you to stay alive. God wants to keep you alive, so that you will experience new life which gifts you with laugher.

REFLECTION QUESTIONS

1) Truth be told, what are areas of bitterness in your life?

2) How have you pushed others away with your bitterness or pain?

3) How would you envision God healing a painful area of your life?

JEWEL 32

Shaking a Plateau
Scriptural Meditation: Proverbs 12:1

We run, walk, Zumba, and count calories to drop the pounds. If you have been successful on this journey, you have likely found yourself trying to shake a weight loss plateau. I once lost 60 pounds naturally and then maintained a 45-pound weight-loss for three years.

Before I fell completely off the wagon and regained the weight, I spent nearly a year at a plateau. The scale would not move as I continued making changes to my diet and exercise regimen. And when the scale did move, it displayed weight gain. I had hit a plateau!

One day while grocery shopping, I came across a sheet titled "Tips for shaking off those weight loss plateaus." Desperate for help, I sat in my car and began reading. Within minutes, God revealed plateaus apply to more than weight loss. Many of you are experiencing emotional and spiritual plateaus.

The first question asked on the tip sheet was, "Are you eating too many calories?" Calories are needed to supply our bodies with energy, but they weigh us down when we consume too many and avoid exercise. As in the natural, we can ingest too many emotional calories. Are you consuming too much drama, stress, or other people's problems ?

"Are you getting enough calories?" Our bodies can adapt to fewer calories, but we have to make sure that we are getting enough protein to build muscle. After reading the question on calorie intake, I began to consider what happens to our spiritual lives when there is not enough spiritual nourishment to keep us powered up.

Are you getting enough emotional, physical and spiritual protein? Are you getting enough sleep? Are you "dining" out with people who give you positive reinforcement? Are you spending time with people who help you grow spiritually, or are you simply consuming gossip which is better known as unwanted calories? Are you getting a good spiritual Word that will build your spiritual muscles?

"Are you doing the same old exercise routine you started with?" You go to church then back home, then back to church, but there is not the addition of prayer, meditation, or scripture reading.
Are you waiting to be promoted on your job and you have avoided returning to school or building your skill set? Are you praying those "now I lay me down to sleep" prayers when fervent, effectual prayer is necessary? Or, have you simply given up on prayer altogether because you feel things will not change?

According the brochure, weight loss requires steps to regulate metabolism and adjust eating habits. If you are in a spiritual plateau, then changes will have to take place. But if you keep doing what you've always done, you may likely find yourself continuing to pack on "pounds."

REFLECTION QUESTIONS

1) In what areas of your life do you sense a plateau?

2) What are the extra "calories" weighing you down?

3) What changes must you make to shake whatever plateau you have in your life?

JEWEL 33

Favor with God and Man
Scriptural Meditation: 1 Samuel 2:26; Luke 2:52

G ood morning!" I said to the unknown woman wearing a blue dress that reminded me of the Bahamian waters I cruised across on my graduation cruise. The woman wore the dress with confidence and there was purpose in each step. We entered the building together, but I stopped off to the lady's room. After locating the front office, I was escorted to a conference room. Nervously, I entered the room where other speakers were gathered. Again, I encountered the woman with the blue dress who hadn't really acknowledged me earlier.

There I was, a seminarian new to the community invited in to speak before 800 high school girls about womanhood. A teacher, who heard about my preaching from a cousin living in another city, suggested to her principal that I should be invited to speak at the school's inaugural program.

The woman in the ocean-kissed dress greeted others in the room before sitting at the table and beginning a conversation with me.

"So who are you?" I told her my name and that I was a seminarian at Duke Divinity School. I may have even mentioned my church affiliation, but I can't recall. She continued to ponder the information received and looked at the program. "Oh, Dr. Simmons?" she says.

By then I'm wondering where this conversation is headed before she asks: "How did you get here?" Because she had never seen me in her circle or heard me on the radio as she had one of the other speakers, I quickly became a person of interest. While I attempted to be gracious and respectful as I answered her questions, I simply wanted to reply, "God!"

It was the favor of God that had provided access to that space and opportunity. God granted me favor with men and women who created the opportunity for me to speak into the lives of future mothers, wives, politicians, chemists, educators, and world changers.

When you have favor with God and man, people will ask "Why are you here?" Sometimes you won't even know the answer. God may have you on an assignment no public relations team could have orchestrated; an assignment no branding strategist could even design or launch. With God's favor, doors once previously closed are opened and the Holy Spirit summons a spiritual concierge service to assist with your needs.

The following day, a quote from my message was included in the local paper. As a media historian, that article captured a moment in my ministry that someone may one day note for the historical record. On that day, the honorarium was a biscuit and some water, but the true payment was operating in the favor and will of God.

REFLECTION QUESTIONS

1) How has God favored you by opening doors?

2) How did you know you received the favor of God?

3) How has God used you to show favor to someone else?

JEWEL 34

Sowing Into the Future
Scriptural Meditation: Proverbs 13:22

The parable of the prodigal son is a familiar story even applicable to our contemporary circumstances and lives. The story found in Luke 15:11-32 helps us understand that like the God in the Old Testament was committed to Israel, the God of the New Testament is just as concerned and in love with us even when we choose to go astray. While some of us find it interesting that the son had the boldness to ask for his inheritance, I was amazed that he had the nerve to even think an inheritance existed. If we were to apply this parable to our contemporary society, the father might have told the younger son: "Nothing from nothing leaves nothing, son!"

I've seen parents call their children in college to request the student send money home from their refund checks and work study jobs. One day, a student explained her mother called her to pay a light bill created by three adults while she was away at college. Sadly, for her and so many others, there is no assistance and likely no inheritance.

Even as a single person without children, I often think about what kind of inheritance I will leave the world. In addition to the natural, there is a spiritual inheritance of faith I desire to pass on.

Have you considered the inheritance you will leave your children and/or communities?

Will your family members have to collect donations through crowdfunding to provide you a decent burial? Or would you leave behind liquid assets or investments so they could pay for your funeral and endow a scholarship or make a contribution to help expand the church you served in life?

Once upon a time, I would not be able to leave a mall or store without purchasing something. I may have worn an outfit a time or two, but what if I could have paid down my debt or invested those funds? Beyond a "that's pretty" there was no long term value.

Fancy things are nice to own, but not at the expense that they own us and leave our families in debt. Instead of leaving things no one will wear again, I pray to leave something that helps someone still on the journey. My prayer is that God will see if he can get it to me, then others will be blessed through me!

REFLECTION QUESTIONS

1) How would you describe yourself as a steward of financial resources?

2) What areas of your finances could you better manage?

3) What changes are you willing to make to ensure you leave something behind for future generations?

JEWEL 35

Friendly Risk-taking
Scriptural Meditation: Proverbs 17:17

With Facebook allowing us to describe relationships as "complicated" or designate "friends" as "acquaintances," it is not surprising that we are involved in countless inauthentic relationships. Someone I consider a friend once told me she doesn't trust anyone. Immediately I thought: Where does this leave our relationship? Does that mean you don't even trust me?

While Christ is the ultimate friend, the example of friendship that encourages me the most is the story of the paralyzed man in Luke 5:17-20. His healing depended on a few good friends. Jesus was in Capernaum, and because so many people had gathered at the place where he preached, the man's four friends realized that the only way to get him to Jesus would be to open the roof and lower the man into the dwelling. Jesus recognized the faith of his friends, and healed the paralyzed man because of that faith.

Do you have friends who would do the unthinkable to help you secure a blessing?

When I landed my first professional job interview in Eden, North Carolina, my friend and sorority sister, Shana, agreed to travel with me to the backwoods. Back then, there was no Google Maps or Mapquest, just Shana reading a Map and looking for the mammoth American flag that I was told would be our landmark. I screamed at Shana for about an hour because we were lost and she could not read the map.

While my other friends would have told me where to put my map, Shana just searched in silence. Did I mention it was about 95 degrees and my 1990 Geo Prizm had no air conditioning?

When I moved four times in five years, Shana participated in three of those experiences and even found herself crawling into a dumpster when I moved at the beginning of 2000. In the process of throwing away boxes, I mistakenly threw my keys in the receptacle that contained the remnants of New Year's Day meals. I will never forget that big pan of barbecue sauce I encountered when searching outside of the can.

Darkness hovered as we tossed things around in the dumpster before one of my new neighbors discovered us and returned with a flashlight. "Clank," we heard the keys but could not find them. After identifying the area where they may have landed, Shana agreed to crawl into the discarded buffet of holiday food and everyday trash. One leg after the other until her entire body was in. I stood by directing the rescue and recovery effort. "Praise the Lord!" We found the keys after an hour of dumpster diving.

Before that day, I knew Shana was a dedicated friend who likely had to keep remembering Paul's words "Love is patient, love is kind" as she navigated the world alongside me. Sadly, Shana later found a bruise on her thigh. Thankfully, she had recently gotten a Tetanus shot! Friendship can be risky business, but it is a blessing worth the risk.

REFLECTION QUESTIONS

1) What are the character traits of a good friendship?

2) How would you describe the friendship you offer to people in your life? How would they describe the friendship received from you?

3) What could you do to become a better friend?

JEWEL 36

Under the Influence of Faith

Scriptural Meditation: Matthew 17:20

Walking by faith is often a journey filled with missteps and cracks in the sidewalk. It is, most times, done in isolation as we walk alone. Yes, there will be friends and loved ones who understand what you are endeavoring to do. However, there will be many who can't understand what may look "craycray." You know, just foolish. Noah-foolish.

Abraham-foolish. Hannah-drunk-in-love with God's power foolish. Woman-with-the-issue-of-blood-crawling-on-the-ground-foolish. Foolish because you believe and declare one thing when circumstances indicate another. I am finding that God may not do a "big reveal" in your life until you start to look and feel like a fool.

Preachers and prophets confirm words from the Lord, but a word directly from God will have you crossing over seas onto dry land. God can even speak through those who are not in ministry. But when there are too many voices in the mix, you may not be able to detect when God is speaking. Without a prayer life and times of stillness, your faith may be dependent on emotions or circumstances.

On your faith journey, you may have researched the route and made travel arrangements, and then God says "go this way." But, God, that route won't work because I have MapQuested it in the spirit. I believe I should stay the course and take Exit 40. But you want me to take Exit 20 and take the rest of the journey through the woods and possibly cross over a creek? Now that doesn't make any sense!

No, the course God might send you on may not make much sense.

"Faith operates when [a situation] is out of control," said the International First Lady Co-Pastor Susie Owens in a sermon during the 85th Mt. Calvary Holy Church Convocation.

Out of control is when you are on that journey I referenced and somewhere between Exit 30 and 40 you find yourself at a dead end with no highway in sight. Out of control when you find your car stalled and you are without gas. Your mobile phone is out of range so you can't call AAA to rescue you. You find yourself driving in blinding rain while on a two-lane highway where the lanes have disappeared. Yes, for a few miles, hours, days, or even months you find yourself having nothing to depend on but God. You stay in the car and call on the name of Jesus! "Lord, if you don't get me there, I won't make it." There is fear and possibly the discomfort of danger crouching at your door. If you get out of the car, you will get drenched from the rain on the outside.

"Faith is sometimes uncomfortable and hard," a friend recently reminded me.

Yet even in the midst of that rock and hard place, I have enough faith to believe that God is there! On those days when I want to abort the mission and hitchhike to a comfortable place, I remember that the one who initiated the mission is faithful.

Oh, I'm still trying to make it to my Exit 40, but I just keep driving, slowing down when necessary and accelerating when opportunity permits. I'll get there. By faith I will!

REFLECTION QUESTIONS

1) How do you know when fear has accelerated past faith in your life?

2) When a situation was out of control, how do you recall faith taking over?

3) What are indicators in your life that your faith has grown?

JEWEL 37

Ready, Set, Go!
Scriptural Meditation: Luke 21:36

Oh, I'm just sitting here on this couch...okay. Oh, I heard about that. What time does it start? Okay, bye!"

As she ends the phone conversation, she slowly gets up to avoid falling and then proceeds to the bathroom. Minutes, later, she is dressed and putting on lip stick and changing purses to fit the occasion.

I often say I am like my granny when it comes to receiving a last-minute invitation. If she has no other plans, you can call her and within a matter of minutes, she can get ready for lunch, a church service, a funeral, or a trip to the mall. As a young woman, I learned that one should always have a few essential items in an effort to stay prepared for anything. A woman should have an inventory of pantyhose, a black dress, white suit, pair of black shoes with a good heel, some pearls and any other items necessary for your lifestyle. From my grandfather, I learned not to go out with your shoes looking any old kind of way. Even if they are old, you need to replace the heel and give them a good shine. While I have definitely fallen short on the shoe rule, I am grateful for the tidbits you can't learn on television shows about fashion and style.

I once casually discussed breaking bread with an associate, but did not think the invite would come so soon. I responded and indicated that I could meet thirty minutes later than suggested. Thankfully, the other party called to confirm. I had a few hours warning, so I completed my tasks and started to consider what to wear. Just like granny, I threw an outfit together (I even ironed), pinned up my hair, dabbed on a little mid-week makeup and I was "rehd to go." Granny's principle was at play: always be prepared. After returning home and considering how quickly I was able to get ready for the impromptu date, I realized how so many people miss their moment by being unprepared.

Would you be ready if the opportunity you desired presented itself?

Would your resume be ready if your dream job posted within the next 24 hours?

Would you have a passport if you received a last-minute invite to sail the Mediterranean?

Would your business plan be ready if your personal banker called offering a new loan with zero percent interest?

Would your soul be ready if Jesus returned today? 2 Peter 3:10 reminds us: "But the day of the Lord will come like a thief..."

Would you need to primp and clean yourself up, or would you be "rehd to go"?

So often, we receive spiritual text messages prompting us to get ready, yet we ignore them, erase the messages, or simply power down. They will not disappear. Like messages in the natural, that little mailbox symbol will just sit there until you listen or read the message.

REFLECTION QUESTIONS

1) What has the spirit been leading you to prepare for?

2) Have you been told to prepare for the shifting of a season in your life?

3) Have you encouraged others in your sphere of influence to prepare?

JEWEL 38

Babies, Fools, and Angels
Scriptural Meditation: Luke 4:10-11

The unknown man screamed, *"PEACHES, PEACHES, "* as he banged on the door of my first apartment. "Who?" I answered trying to peep through the window without being seen. "Peaches!"

"No, you have the wrong apartment." Because there were few visitors to my rural North Carolina home, I was a tad shaken. Later that week, I visited the barber shop behind my unit and told the barbers about the encounter. A police officer owned the shop which served as a Welcome Center for a newcomer like myself. There I would inquire about people I met around town and about things I would never learn from my colleagues. I learned I was presently living in an apartment where drugs were previously dealt. And if that wasn't enough, the empty lot of land across from my apartment building was a crack house that had burned down. Guess the property management company I visited with my parents and grandmother forgot to mention those few details.

Fast forward the following year after relocating. Before there was a www.blackpeoplemeet.com, people connected via telephone and newspaper advertisements to date and meet mates. For example, during a phone interview for an article I was writing for my job as a newspaper reporter, I was asked on a date. I was 23 years old and intrigued by our conversation. We had mutual associates and his work required state government clearance. While his background checked out, the location of our initial date needed further investigation. We ventured to an undergraduate party of his fraternity only to find ourselves running hand-in-hand out of the building during a shootout.

"Arlecia!" A voice called out as I stopped running. While I stopped to identify who had called, my date ran to the car and was preparing to leave. Thankfully, the car had to warm up. Had it not been winter, I may have been left. We were able to laugh about it later, but that incident was no laughing matter.

Years later at the S.C. State Fair, my interviewee-turned-date introduced me to his wife. "Do you remember that date I told you about?" She laughed as the three of us recounted the date with a stranger that ended during a shootout at the Armory. That story could have ended with the headline: "Journalist and Social Worker Wounded During Fraternity Party."

Incidents such as the above remind me quite clearly, if it had not been the Lord on my side, where would I be? Being an adventurer has led me into known and unknown threats. During those times, I am reminded of the saying "God takes care of babies and fools." I would add "and everyone else in between."

Many times I have found myself in the fool category, living life on the edge where the sidewalk ends. Thankfully, God responded to my mama or grandfather's prayers to keep angels encamped around me. Before I knew to request their presence, angels watched over me and some accrued overtime.

So often we go about our lives taking God's protection for granted. Others died on roads we travel yet we were spared. As I consider the places I have journeyed and the times when I could have been taken out, I tell God "thank you" for giving me another chance to complete my assignment.

REFLECTION QUESTIONS

1) When and where have you felt God's protection?

2) How do you acknowledge God's protection?

3) If you had to describe God's protection, what are some of the words you would use?

JEWEL 39

Struggle in Disguise
Scriptural Meditation: Psalm 37:25

On social networking, it is common to see a hashtag with the words "the struggle," or statements such as "the struggle is real." For many who are experiencing hardships, it is difficult to mask the actual struggle. For the homeless people we rush by because of their stench, the struggle is indeed real. Yet, there is likely a sister at work you didn't realize also comes to work from a shelter. But before the shelter, she bathed herself and her children in the bathrooms of hotel lobbies. She realized if she visited different hotels throughout the month, workers and guests would not know she had never checked in. Her life mirrors the story of Chris Gardner whose struggles we learned about in the movie *Pursuit of Happyness*.

Like this mother and Gardner, many of you go through life masking struggles of varying degrees.

Someone once told me: "You make struggle look easy." It is likely I have during those seasons where I strived to not look like what I was going through. Struggle and easy were two words that did not go together when I checked my memory. I reflected back to early 1997 when I worked in Eden, N.C., as the lifestyles writer at a local newspaper. It was my first job out of college and after taxes I brought home about $292 a week. My rent was $290 a month and once I asked the property management company if I could pay $280 and pay the balance later. The remaining $10 would have allowed me to buy some groceries or gas, possibly make it to the next pay period. I was a new college graduate who hadn't quite figured out how to pay what I considered "big bills."

In that job I won a third place award from the North Carolina Press Association. I struggled as a young writer, but I kept working hard. I won the only award received by my paper, so I traveled alone to Chapel Hill, N.C., to receive my award. I charged some gas on a credit card and remembered not even having enough money to buy a new pair of pantyhose. (This may explain why I buy multiple pairs now.)

I was gifted a new outfit for Christmas, so I wore it and prayed no one would see the stockings with runs and holes. My skirt was long, so I proudly walked across the stage at the University of North Carolina at Chapel Hill to receive the award I earned for writing about a nudist ranch. Yep, I went and did a story as people walked around "nek-hed."

Deep inside I was embarrassed, but runs or not, I was going to be recognized with other journalists in the state. There were so few people of color in the audience, but it didn't matter. I was proud to be there.

Even with holes in my stockings, I was walking by faith and not by sight. Although 22 years old, I knew my circumstances wouldn't always be like this.

It would not be the first time someone had lived with such a sacrifice, as many of our foremothers did the same as they made ways out of no ways. For those privileged to have multiples of necessary items, we may forget or never know how it feels to experience a deficit.

While struggle may look easy to onlookers, it can be painful, embarrassing, and destructive to our psyches. But when you know who you are and whose you are, you can walk through any situation with boldness and wait until your change comes.

REFLECTION QUESTIONS

1) In what ways do you make struggle look easy?

2) What have you learned from life's struggles?

3) Why are we ashamed to share our struggles with others?

JEWEL 40

Just Trying to Get My Water

Scriptural Meditation: John 4:1-30

Have you ever tried to avoid eye contact with someone to avoid an unwanted conversation? You acted busy and diverted your eyes, but they still found a way to intercept you.

The woman at the well in John 4 was simply trying to get her water when a Jew named Jesus intruded her gaze. The woman came to the well later in the day to likely avoid others who deemed her life more jacked up than their narratives.

As I read this text, I looked into the well and saw my own reflection. And yes, I know depending on who preaches this text and how it is interpreted you'll walk away with a variety of thoughts about this woman. By talking to her, Jesus crosses major boundaries of religion, ethnicity and gender. She meets Jesus in the middle of the day while in the previous chapter there was a Pharisee named Nicodemus who met Jesus at night. Nicodemus is an insider but as a Samaritan she is an outsider, religiously, socially and politically. If I take it a step further as I compare and contrast, Nicodemus' story in John 3 can also be considered a "call narrative." He comes to Jesus, recognizes he is from God and asks "How can a man be born again when he is old." Jesus welcomes the conversation and the question, and calls him in to relationship by responding, "You must be born again." Oh, but Nicodemus couldn't quite wrap his mind around how you go from womb birth to spirit birth.

Jesus was not talking about amniotic fluid; rather, he was talking about being born of water and spirit through Baptism. We, too, can find ourselves in a quandary when God speaks to us through earthly examples. When we can't translate the parable or oracle, we may enter into theological debates with God.

You don't have to go to divinity school or seminary to do theology. We all do some kind of theology.

In John 4 this woman shares her own theology about worship when Jesus asks for a simple drink of water. But we learn that Jesus is asking for so much more from this woman and from each of us.

Like this unnamed woman I had to ask some questions. But Jesus is never afraid of our questions and he often begins the conversations. I mean, what are you really asking for here, Jesus? I am just trying to get my water.

You know, I'm just trying to have the career I planned. I consulted you and you let me go to college and get these here degrees, and now you are asking me for a drink?

Okay, okay, I will give you a sip and I'll let my light shine by writing about people's faith in those stories I've been called to write, and when the missionary society at the Mt. Sinai Missionary Baptist church calls and asks me to be their Saturday morning speaker I'll do that, but remember… I'm just trying to get my water.

Okay, okay, I'll work at two Christian colleges but I didn't go there to spiritually influence people. I came to write these here press releases, take a few pictures and then teach some media and communications classes and every now and then when a student asks if I'm saved I won't act like I'm in the witness protection program, but I didn't come here to evangelize... I'm really just trying to get my water...

Okay, okay, I'll talk with the girls in the dorm about how their bodies are a temple and that means they can't just use them and abuse them in exchange for Coach purses. While I'm in Orangeburg, S.C., I'll even work in a newly established ministry. I'll help with the media, and get them on the radio; I'll do the morning announcements and serve as the exhorter.

I will tell your people, "Lift up your heads , O ye gates', even lift them ye everlasting doors; and the King of glory shall come in." I'll remind them that you are the King of Glory but note I'm really just trying to get my water.

Okay, okay, I'll exhort and speak at prayer breakfasts, conduct workshops, and keynote banquets. I'll even be a bootleg preacher every now and then; whenever you need me, send me and I'll go.

But you can't possibly want me to preach and teach your Gospel, like, all the time? I mean, my money is already funny and my change is already strange. I don't have many friends, but you mean to tell me now you want to set me further apart? Leave what I know for what I don't know? I'm just trying to get my water.

Sir "you have nothing to draw with and the well is deep."
Sir, not only am I a woman, but I have some dry and desolate places in my own life.

I really don't have any water to give or share. I mean, do you really know who I am?

Like the woman Jesus meets at the well, I've had my own man problems.

If I give you what you're asking for I may never get one.

I'm just trying to get my water.

And after hearing me out, I heard Jesus respond: the water I give will saturate every dry place in your life.

After being intercepted at the well called academic training, I dropped all that I had originally pursued to answer the call of ministry and tell a thirsty world about the living water called Jesus Christ.

REFLECTION QUESTIONS

1) What have you thirsted after and obtained only to find you remained parched and unsatisfied?

2) What represents the water pots you had to drop in order to pursue a greater purpose?

3) What is Jesus requesting from you today?

EPILOGUE

My Soul Looks Back and Reflects

Scriptural Meditation: Psalm 37: 25

As I prepared to celebrate my 40th birthday on May 26, 2014, I considered what I would have liked to have known at age 20. There are some things I had to go through for my journey and testimony, but there were other things someone could have warned me about.

I pray you are blessed by the jewels from my treasure:

1) Enjoy the life you have been given. No matter the time or financial resources, figure out how to enjoy your time in the land of the living. If it's nothing more than taking a few minutes watching birds, do it! Spend time with people who make you smile! If joy can only come from big experiences, then life will leave you exhausted. Find joy and happiness in small things.

2) Consult the Lord in all things. Pray often and fervently. Choose relationship over religion. Religion says "go to church on Sunday," but relationship says "transform into the church each day." Find ways to connect with God on a consistent basis.

3) Buy quality clothes and shoes. It may sound old fashioned, but always have a black and white suit or dress. Keep something to wear to a banquet or evening event. You never know, you may just be asked to speak. Stay prepared to "be presentable."

4) Fruits and vegetables: Eat them regularly so you can have good skin, stamina, and health.

5) Go to the doctor and choose health care providers wisely. Don't allow a personality clash to allow you to end up with thousands of dollars in dental care. Just find another dentist. Invest in your health the same way you invest in your car or home.

6) Avoid friends who make life seem like you're a character in a movie that's about the Witness Protection Program. A friendship should be one of mutual respect and transparency. Realize that friendships come packaged in different ways and may even have seasons.

7) Invest in yourself. Whether it is education, vacation, or a daytrip to the spa, spend money and time building up and replenishing yourself. Life and the people in it will use every ounce in your bucket (if you let them); so refill it often!

8) Take risks. If you stay on the fence continually wondering "what will happen if I…" you'll likely remain on that fence longer than necessary. By the time you make a move, the fence will have rusted and you will have an infection. God gave us free will for a reason.

9) Welcome friendships that make no sense to the natural eye. My friends from different cultures and generations have blessed my life in countless ways, including those who offer "happy thoughts" instead of "Fada God" prayers. Those are the friendships that help lead me into a greater life of faithfulness. Be open to different perspectives. You don't have to embrace them all, but being aware of them will strengthen your own.

10) Forgive often and quickly. If you are not careful, most of your life can be spent drafting a "sic 'em" list. While Christians are encouraged to pray for our enemies, you can find yourself spending more energy asking God to sic 'em like a big, mean dog. While you are carrying the baggage of unforgiveness, they have packed a few bags and gone about their lives on a cruise to Bahamas and Mexico. They have pics on Instagram while you are home lamenting in unforgiveness.

11) Learn how to keep some secrets. There are just some things that should remain between you and God. Or in the words of my granny and a few others, "Never let the right hand know what the left hand is doing." While transparency is important in intimate relationships, some people use our secrets to build cases against us. Sadly, there is no statute of limitations on ratchet disclosure.

12) Learn how to cook. I didn't say you have to become Gina Neely, but learn how to cook so you can feed yourself. Learn how to cook so you

can share table fellowship with your friends. If nothing else, learn how to cook one meat, one vegetable, one starch, and one dessert. When there is a potluck, just rotate categories. Seriously, it will save you money and keep you safe.

13) Tell the truth. Lying leaves you exhausted. While not everyone will be able to digest your truth, try to remain on the right side of right at all times. Recently, someone asked if I was tired of my braids. I simply told them: "No. I just don't have any money to get my hair done." I know that's not what a woman of faith should have said, but I was honest. I could have lied about my hair needing a break, but why lie about something so trivial? Lies require you to keep them all straight.

14) Help somebody. Avoid being a leech. If your hand is always out to receive but never in a position to give, you'll miss many blessings. Help a child, help an elderly neighbor, help an enemy, and help someone who is in no position to return the assistance.

15) Don't allow your insecurities to stop you from getting to know people or experience new things. In high school, my English teacher had me recite a poem titled "Desiderata." I will always remember the stanza: "If you compare yourself with others, you may become vain and bitter; for always there will be greater and lesser persons than yourself."

16) Lift as you climb. If someone opens a door for you, open a door for someone else. Find someone to mentor or help along the journey.

17) Treasure family, even the ones who get on your last nerves. A time will come when they will not be there for that nerve. Ask your older rela-

tives questions about your people. Find out "who you be" by listening and gathering.

18) Discover a passion. Find something that keeps you awake at night. A hobby, a vocation, a special community project, or a dream you pray will come to fruition.

19) Save a little something but don't hoard it all. Find a way to always have a little something during lean days. Strive to pay your bills on time which will ensure you will have more to save, share, and spend. Maintain integrity with your business dealings.

20) Do you! Never be afraid to be your authentic self. (Now, if you ever find yourself on an episode of Cheaters singing "I bust the windows out your car" then ignore this one if it characterizes your authenticity.) Never flip your switch to off just because those around you haven't identified their power source. Be smart. Be bold. Be revolutionary. Be you.

21) Be okay with having a Rudolph anointing. He never got to join in any reindeer games. He never got an invite to the cookout. He listened as they planned the dinner he wasn't invited to attend. There are people who are ordained to be in our public lives, but can't have access to our private lives. Being alone may be a season, or you may just never be invited to reindeer games. Shine, anyway.

22) Don't be so serious all the time. Laugh. Laugh at yourself. Laugh when you want to cry. Learn how to tell a good (appropriate) joke.

23) Stop trying to keep up with the Joneses. Remember, their mail is now being forwarded to a new address since their foreclosure. Clothing, shoes, and other fancy things can't prove your worth or value. Bragging and comparison will usually indicate your insecurities. Appreciate what you have even while working to obtain more. And when you get more, share.

24) Journal. Write about your journey. Spend a few minutes each day or week writing about the journey. As you write, consider how your faith is being tested or strengthened. One day it may be a way for you to remember how you made it over.

25) Do not be afraid of the unknown. God will hide blessings in unexpected experiences, places, and encounters with complete strangers. You may miss an encounter with angels doing what you have always done.

26) Pay attention to the news. Know about what's going on in your neighborhood and around the globe. While you will often have to filter what you hear and read, seek to understand the changes taking place around you.

27) Stay abreast of your health. "I don't want to know" is the phrase that has landed many Black women in early graves. Lose weight before your knees get to aching; and hear doctors and loved ones when they advise changes for improved health.

28) Plan for the future. Make small goals. If you can't envision yourself getting a degree, then just make a small goal to at least look at the application. Then make a goal to request the transcript. "Fitna' do" something usually leads to never getting it done.

29) Seek out people who are wiser than you, and then stalk them. Well, just joking about the latter. Whether they become a "friend in your head," or someone who agrees to mentor you, ACCEPT the offer! Find time to spend with them.

30) Learn when to speak and when to remain silent. If life was a court-room, most of us would stay in contempt of court. Not everything deserves testimony or cross examination.

31) Learn how to give and receive grace.

32) Avoid drugs and excessive uses of alcohol. Both will decrease the vitality of your body and make you look seasoned before your time. If you find yourself needing to drink until you pass out, consider the possibility that you may need to confront something you are trying to suppress. Find a counselor, doctor, or clergy member to talk with about these issues.

33) When you're single, flirt often. Hey, it helps you keep hope alive. It boosts self-esteem and reaffirms you are "fearfully and wonderfully made." Now what happens after that depends on the circumstances and the subject.

34) Guard your heart. Of course we have skin, tissue and muscle to guard our physical hearts, but you will need to use your brain and spirit to guard from people and experiences that may injure your spirit. Pray for your heart to be guarded against manipulation. Ask for divine direction in every interaction of life. (Refer back to 33)

35) Fellowship with other believers. Always remain friends with "a church girl/boy." They may never be appropriately dressed for the club, but they know how to get a prayer through. Will your conversations be spent gossiping or talking about foolishness, or will they be focused on faith, hope, and love?

36) Don't squander opportunities. There will be times when you have to say "no" to something that appears should be met with a "yes." Remember, for everything there is a season. When it is a "yes" season, walk into it and refrain from being trifling. Yes, I said it, trifling! Give it your all, or allow someone else to give it all they have!

37) Try your best to stay out of the grips of the law. Drive the speed limit, for real. Only write checks you have money to cover, don't transport miscellaneous packages, and stay out of questionable vehicles. If you go into questionable spaces, always know where the exits are. Don't get hemmed up in foolishness that can take your freedom.

38) Love yourself enough to know that love is from God. Love is not manipulative or wasteful of your emotions. Love does not kick or hit or call you out of your name. Love is patient and kind. Love will love you back to life even after you've tapped out.

39) Cookies. If you keep giving out samples they'll never see the value in ordering a few dozens to take home to mama. Catch my drift? (That's old school right there) As you guard your heart, guard your cookies. That is, until the right person demonstrates that they are ready to become a partner in bakery ownership.

40) Give thanks. Thank God for every benefit known and unknown. Thank others when they aid in making your life better. The waitress who brings the extra napkins is worthy of a "thank you." The senior who sacrifices to give you that $5 handshake before you head back to school is worthy of a "thank you." While saying it with your mouth is important, also consider sending cards, notes, or something tangible. Thank teachers, loved ones who prayed, and even those who offered curses God turned into blessings. Give thanks! Thank you makes room for more.

REFLECTION QUESTIONS

1) What are some lessons you have learned over the course of the past 10 years?

2) What words of advice would you give to your younger self?

3) What testimony would you share with someone today?

POSTSCRIPT

To God be the glory for the great things God has done! It's finally done, ya'll!

While completing this manuscript, I listened to a YouTube video of Dr. Mattie Nottage whom I learned about via an email. In an interview, she talked about spiritual warfare and how there are forces of darkness sabotaging and halting those things God has assigned for us to do.

Thankfully, the imps on that assignment were reassigned so I could release these words I pray will heal someone. I pray you laughed. I pray my words made you think. I pray gifts inside of you were stirred as you read these simple words.

Through the stories I have shared, I pray you are released to share your own. My prayer is that you will begin to dig deep for your own treasure and work to tell your story. Whether you are telling your stories from behind prison walls or in a nook in your kitchen, it's likely life has given you a jewel to share on this journey.

I leave you with a word from 1 Chronicles 16:24 (NLT):

"Publish his glorious deeds among the nations. Tell everyone about the amazing things he does."

AUTHOR BIO

The Rev. Dr. Arlecia D. Simmons began her professional career as a newspaper reporter, but now communicates on God's behalf. She is an award-winning journalist, a playwright, an inspirational speaker and writer, and a member of Delta Sigma Theta Sorority, Inc. Simmons is the Chief Encourager of Look 'n Live Ministries, Inc., which was birthed to fulfill the assignment of encouraging people to lead abundant and faithful lives.

Simmons earned a Bachelor of Arts in Mass Communication from Winthrop University and a Master of Arts in Journalism from the University of South Carolina. In December 2009, she earned a Doctor of Philosophy degree in Mass Communications from the University of Iowa while completing her first semester at Duke University Divinity School. She graduated from Duke in May 2012, and was ordained to Christian ministry on Pentecost Sunday, May 27, 2012. Her ordination is endorsed by the American Baptist Churches USA.

Simmons enjoys educating people about the unique Gullah culture that shaped her identity.

To book Rev. Dr. Arlecia D. Simmons for speaking engagements, workshops, or writing projects, e-mail her at looknlive@gmail.com Visit her online at www.looknlive.com